Time Capsule of a Costa Rican Kidnapping

a memoir

By John P. Murphy

Flat World Publishing

Puerto Escondido, Mexico

2015

Copyright 2015 by John P. Murphy

All rights Reserved. No part of this publication may be reproduced, stored in a retrieval system, or transmitted in any form or by any means, electronic, mechanical, photocopying, recording or otherwise, without the prior permission of the copyright owner.

Flat World Publishing
Puerto Escondido, Mexico

First Edition June 2015

This is a work of creative nonfiction. The events are portrayed to the best of John P. Murphy's memory. While all the stories in this book are true, some names and identifying details have been changed to protect the privacy of the people involved.

ISBN: *978-1511807333*

To Ian, Ben and Hannah.

With Love,

Papá

Mexico, 2015

Contents

Introduction..v

A Note on the Reading.......................vi

Part One: The First Pilgrimage....................1

Part Two: You Can't Make People Happy....53

Part Three: End of the Pilgrim................127

Part Four: Costa Rican Justice................154

Part Five: The Second Pilgrimage............204

Part Six: Escape from Costa Rica............245

Afterword...289

Introduction

There is no life without suffering; emotional pain visits everyone at some point. It is the human condition.

We all get an unequal share, but for reasons only known to your god and the universe, it is a fair share.

How we manage our lives amid this emotional pain makes all the difference.

Five years ago, when my wife kidnapped our three young children, I drove them all to the airport.

I got my share of suffering and I am not alone, there are roughly 200,000 children kidnapped by a family member in the U.S. each year.

This book started as a time capsule memoir, to protect my story from the lazy memory of historical revisionism. The writing has since laid waste to blame, and now serves as a vehicle for self-recovery.

I lay no claim to innocence. I am neither angel nor devil. Like most people, most times, I fall somewhere in the middle.

There are lyrical snapshots included of my time as a father, when I was teaching, and my three children were under seven and above the poverty line. That has all changed, but the memories remain the same.

I am calling out to Ian, Ben and Hannah. I am hoping they will hear me.

My journey affirms the perfection of the universe, where amid prolonged personal disaster, a life worth celebrating emerges and dreams become reality, in ways we never imagined.

If you are reading this now, a dream has been realized.

A Note on the Reading:

An asterisk (*) indicates information not known to John P. Murphy at the time, but later provided by Dan Knight in 2014 through interviews, personal emails, airline receipts, wire transfer receipts and photographs. You will find the first reference to this on page 58.

Part I
The First Pilgrimage
30 July 2011
Chapter 1: The Vision.

The butterflies were passing and clouds hung low on a Saturday morning in Costa Rica when I walked past the park in Jaco Beach. Young mothers gathered small children to walk a mini-pilgrimage from the park to the Catholic Church where I attended mass regularly and sat next to old leathery Ticos with straight backs and chubby wives: men who still drive the same Range Rover they bought from the dealership in 1976; a united nations of prostitutes share the same pews as shop owners with their pretty wives and clean children. Taxi drivers, who worked all night and bathed in cologne, numbered among the faithful. In community, we sought redemption.

I go to church for the same reason I go to the opera: to find God amid the art and the humanity; for the silence between the noise; to sit anonymous among others practicing piety and reverence; where silence passes for participation. Both offer fertile ground for sowing meditative thoughts, where cat naps are disguised as deep thought or deep prayer.

I was raised Catholic, but am of eclectic taste in religions: I believe some of all but not all of any.

I prayed Hail Mary's in abundance to be reunited with my children; that my wife, the Costa Rican Justice System, God or The Universe would allow me to realize that goal. I am sure God was helping; I just hadn't yet seen any results. The end result of God's plan is near impossible to envision when stuck in the middle, face down in the dark, with hands tied behind. There is little hope of salvation and even less of redemption in those moments of solitude and desperation where faith is tested and character revealed.

Family Court Procedure in Costa Rica can be slowed by appeals and procedures for years, during which time there is no contact between father and child. Every day was another day of uncertainty: there was no clear vision of a common future in what felt like a state sanctioned kidnapping. I felt helpless, abused. Gatekeepers stood round my children, access to their father was denied.

Given the circumstances, how could I express the beliefs and values that represent my character? How do I express my desire to be present in the everyday lives of my children? What action can I take to highlight the injustice of justice delayed? How do I disrupt the systematic norm in an acceptable manner?

I toyed with but rejected the following possibilities:

1. Silently sit outside the courthouse every day until given the right to speak with my children.
2. After six months without contact, add hunger strike to option number one.
3. Get myself a massive tattoo of the Spanish word "Dolor," across my back. "Dolor" means pain.
4. Get famous singing Beethoven's Ode to Alegria in the Catholic Churches of San Jose, Costa Rica.

I'd only prove I was another crazy gringo, a difficult stereotype to shake. I wanted to make a testament to commitment and an expression of profound emotional pain. Even the modest Civil Disobedience of sitting silently would be considered aggressive in a country with no standing army.

Legal counsel strongly recommended: "Do nothing, because anything you do will be used against you as proof that you are just another crazy gringo." Costa Ricans believe most gringos are aggressive, pushy and crazy. All of Latin America believes most gringos are aggressive and crazy for one reason or another. In general most people in the world don't like us.

I cried watching the young families start their mini-pilgrimage, but through the tears I discovered a means to express my pain. I decided to become a pilgrim and walk to the basilica of Cartago. Being a pilgrim meant walking along the hot coastal plain, over the wet curvy mountains and down the dangerous highway to enter the Central Valley. Total distance: about 100 hard walking miles.

I had never considered a pilgrimage; I didn't know the challenges or the risks. I only knew that in this Catholic country, walking for four days and nights to visit a small piece of charcoal around which a church was built would not be considered an act of mental instability.

I calculated while making arrangements; the feast day of the patron saint of Costa Rica was in four days, with four long walks I could make it to see the Little Black Virgin right on time.

Chapter 2: The Little Black Virgin.

In the year 1639, near Cartago, Costa Rica, a little girl found a three inch piece of rock that resembles the image of the Virgin Mary, except this rock was black, so the Virgin of Los Angeles is commonly known as, "La Negrita," (The Little Black Virgin).

The rock wasn't so special when the girl arrived home and showed it to her mom. The rock became more special when it escaped from the house during the night and returned to where the girl had found it.

The little girl told her priest, and he locked that statue in a box, but this was a Virgin Houdini because the next day that little statue was back in its original place. The Church declared a miracle and built the Basilica of Our Lady of the Angels.

The feast day of the Patron Saint of Costa Rica, La Negrita is August 2 and is celebrated with a pilgrimage. People walk from all parts of the country to visit the little black chunk of carbon. Most folk take a bus into San Jose and walk the pilgrimage from that point, which is a good 6 hour walk to the basilica in Cartago. It is a lesser known of the religious pilgrimages in the world. The Muslims used to walk to Mecca (now they fly commercial jets and it still counts) to earn their Haji cap and the Spaniards have the 1,400 mile Path of Santiago of which Paul Coelho writes, and then the English have Chaucer fame: The Canterbury Tales, which marks with satire the paths of the righteous in Middle English times.

I have made two pilgrimages to The Virgin of the Angels. This story starts with my first pilgrimage and my first epiphany. Four days of solitude and thoughtful suffering revealed the message from within. My body arrived where my mind wanted to be. And that is when she spoke to me.

Chapter 3: Becoming a Pilgrim.

Day One
Jaco to Orotina

10am – 9pm

Total Time: 11 hours

The question was not, "If it is going to rain," the question was, "When is it going to rain on me?" Tropical rain, with drops like frying pans, would eventually visit me on my journey. I bought a yellow slicker set just for the jacket. I also bought a fluorescent reflector vest.

I packed a small backpack with an extra pair of sneakers, long sleeve white button down shirts and my hat. With socks and underwear and sunscreen in abundance, I set off on the road. I phoned two friends to let them know that I was walking to Cartago and that I would check-in with them at night. The roads are dangerous, more dangerous than I imagined, and I wanted someone to know whether I was alive.

I shouldered my relatively light (20 pounds) pack and walked no more than 300 yards when my shoulders and back started to ache from the weight of the pack. I laughed out loud. I had travelled not a quarter of a mile and I was already in pain. I figured I would just have to get used to it. The fun of this journey ended there, 300 yards from the house. Uncle Mike taught my children and I about "the edge of fun," when we went on a pilgrimage with him. We were going to find alligators.

On the Edge of Fun with Uncle Mike

Since I can remember visiting Florida, people have said that there are alligators "everywhere." I had been to Florida a bunch of times and everywhere I looked, there was never an alligator. I wanted to find "everywhere" and meet all the alligators that reside there.

Uncle Mike said he could find a gator for us. We first drove to, "Gator Land," but it was closed on a Sunday.

We drove down some more long straight brown and barren low scrub roads until we arrived at a green state park. Uncle Mike would come here to run in the morning when he was out for 12 and 15 mile courses.

The Park was a series of 17 berms (a mound or wall of earth or sand -Merriam-Webster, 2013) used to filter water. It is an environmentally sustainable project. I had a friend whose father had a Bio sustainable farm in Costa Rica. He used berms like Chinese rice paddies with multiple levels of water filtration with large brightly colored coy that loved to munch on the biodegradable detritus from cooking. You could throw in all the banana peels, coffee grounds and vegetable rinds you wanted. Those coy just ate it all up: a sustainable aqua-compost heap. The berms in this park filter water for the surrounding communities.

For our trip in search of gators we sunblocked, carried water and chose walking sticks along the way. Hats provided shade and we would find a gator that day.

The mid-morning Florida sun rained down hard that first mile into the trail. Sean was almost five and Ted was three and a half. We veered off walking the edge of the lake and followed a shady path into the woods. Hundreds of spider webs dazzled dewy in the morning light. Shadows cast from above revealed the secrets of what lay atop the large translucent palm leaves: spiders and small frogs, leaves, sticks and butterflies.

The world turned to bright lights again; we exited the shade to forge ahead to the less visited areas of the lake where privacy seeking gators may lie. I carried Ted for some of the way. We had been hydrating and sweating for over an hour when Uncle Mike revealed that his family has accused him of pushing outings past "the edge of fun" where the trip becomes not worth the effort.

We weren't concerned with fun or its wavy edges, we were searching for alligators. The success of the experience was not determined by how much "fun" we were having. We didn't blame Uncle Mike for the heat and the long walk; it is easy and fruitless to look outside ourselves for the causes of the situation in which we find ourselves. Forget blame, forget looking outside yourself, responsibility statements start with "I" and end with acceptance.

I applied this process to my own life as I walked on the pilgrimage.

What character flaws kindled this situation? To which personal values did I cleave or cling? These are the questions that cut to the bone of personal development.

People who live in discord with themselves and those around them are vexatious to the spirit. My children: If you don't like your life, then change it. You are the change agent; you are the author of the story of your life.

How do you want that story to be told?

So, we didn't give Uncle Mike a hard time about the "edge of fun," we went with the flow, and that is when we saw an alligator.

She was 12 yards from the shoreline. We first spotted her black eyes above the waterline and the tip of a snout eight inches out front. She submerged; we silently waited until her eyes broke the waterline a few feet away. Uncle Mike crouched cheek to cheek with Ted. He pointed at the gator and Ted followed his finger and they shared the connection and the success. Sean and I crouched and shook with the thrill. Sean and Ted both put fingers to excited mouths and whispered "Shhhh, It's an alligator."

We were eco-adventure scientists that day. We loved life, listening for the sound of a submerged alligator on a hot day in Florida.

We past the edge of fun, on a walk in the woods, with Uncle Mike.

Chapter 4: Emotional Tai Chi.

In the Costa Rica, they use the word, "romeria" to mean a pilgrimage, the Latin root of which means, "those heading towards Rome." Since the pilgrims and a certain species of butterfly travel the roadsides at the end of July, they are both called Romeros, but these butterflies aren't really butterflies, but day flying moths, and I am not really a pilgrim, just a father seeking redemption.

The moths are green and black but the pilgrims come in all shapes and colors and each can be seen by the thousands on any given day. I saw battalions of dead moths on the roadside, victims of hit-and-run accidents the guilty driver probably never knew he had.

I hoped for better luck than all those dead moths because each year at least one pilgrim is martyred.

Walking is glacial slow compared to driving. The entrance road from the coastal highway to Jaco Beach is a little over a mile and takes two minutes to cover by car. After 25 minutes of walking, I was exactly nowhere away from Jaco. This was a journey only accomplished with patience. Frustration is the result of unachieved expectations. Day-to-day garden variety frustrations result from placing time as a determining factor of success. The importance of the process and the perfection of the end result are lost by feeling that we failed the time trial. Spiritual journeys transcend time trial constraints.

Frustration

I have been training for years to become an Emotional Tai Chi Master. I have about a yellow belt now, but with that and some luck, I can extricate myself from just about any emotionally charged situation and escape with my emotions, frustration and dignity intact.

My training in emotional Tai Chi began as an educator, teaching students who didn't want to be taught, then seven years unsuccessfully pursuing my wife's approval and finally as a father serving the needs of three young children. I embarrassed myself repeatedly, falling flat on my face when I allowed my patience fuse to burn past frustration into anger.

The Emotional Tai Chi Master allows energy to pass by without accepting any of the residual negative backwash. Emotional Tai Chi slips punches as the artful dodger of negativity while remaining vigilant to recognize external stimuli triggers that cause the frustration that morphs a discussion into an argument. I practiced sparring and sometimes losing with my wife or students and bosses. I shadowboxed privately until I was fluid with my internal frustrations. I learned when to walk away, and when to run.

The confidence I gained from remaining attentive to my emotions abated my need for approval. I no longer take the anger bait that is so tempting to Brute Irish.

Over the span of seven years of marriage I lost my patience maybe once a year, but each emotional nadir boomeranged on me in the court system of Costa Rica, so I picked apart each event to get to the cause of my behavior. I started at the beginning.

As a child, I chose the worst model ever for managing frustration: The Incredible Hulk.

Other models were thrust upon me, my father was a righteous tough guy, he watched westerns about the cowboy he was, with guys like John Wayne, Clint Eastwood, and Charles Bronson, whose notion of acceptable conflict resolution includes a fair punch in the nose.

My models were brutes. My behavior and management of my frustration was formed on the principles of the Brute Irish American. Brute Irish think hard work and commitment will conquer all. They don't read directions and "If it don't want to fit, make it fit," is an approach used in construction, relationships and putting on pillow cases.

"Just try harder," is the panacea of the practical, the ignorant and the Brute Irish.

Brute Irish drink alcohol in excess then work through hangovers. We are the underdogs. We cry at war movies, wax romantic and quote Shakespeare or Dr. Seuss. We stand tall during the national anthem and glare at disrespectful others. Brute Irish are products of Catholic Education who know their times tables. We don't look for fights, but backing down we don't do so well either.

I have lost more than I could have ever imagined as a result of this Brute Irish approach to life.

I have left that life behind but only after everything I had achieved was burned to the ground. I helped start the fire and once I realized what was happening the blaze was too far gone for me to stop it. Salvation of my former life was not possible, preparing for the rebuild was the only reasonable alternative.

How do we rebuild a life while standing knee deep amid the ashes?

I accepted that I was responsible for each decision that lead me to be alone and sequestered from my children in a foreign land. My situation wasn't the fault of my wife or the courts, no matter how much one lied and the other was so easily manipulated. Blame and guilt are useless tethers to the past and only acceptance cuts the Gordian knot.

I reflected on my past and recognized how each of the choices I made rippled in the pond of my life.

I made proactive moves towards positive change. I clung to my convictions, although those same convictions somehow had allowed me to be sequestered from my children. I kept my faith, told the truth and shamed the devil, hoping that this hard path was temporary and will lead to the greater purpose of my life, that my dreams will be realized if I accept my life as it is, change what I care to and believe the universe will reward my effort. Injustice and chaos were temporary visitors because my life was perfection in repose.

A major cause of frustration was the inequality in my marriage. I desperately sought the approval of my wife. I lacked the confidence to stand up for my beliefs. I acquiesced to her needs in an effort to help my wife find happiness. It is the cross of the easy-going to lie down or retreat to maintain a short-term peace but the long-term results were useless in the personal development of my wife and our relationship together.

Do whatever you have to do to make your wife happy. Forget about personal needs and desires. "Make your wife happy," was my mantra and in allegiance to that belief, I gave everything without prejudice.

Only after slaying the beasts of guilt and blame and then analyzing the events of my past was I able to begin positive change. I wrote, I acted in the best interest of my children, I looked for love and learned to live in the present, unconcerned with the depressive past and the anxiety riddled future.

Chapter 5: Meeting My Wife.

After more than an hour of walking, I arrived at Las Nubes School, the school where I worked when I met my wife eight years before. At that time, I took a trip from Jaco to Manuel Antonio, to visit a friend. We went out to quench our non-existent thirst and to look for love.

Soledad was easy to spot from across the bar in a red knit half-top and white pants. She was strikingly beautiful. She was with Pablo, who was too thin, too handsome and too polished not to be gay, but one never knows with Latino men. Soledad shared eye contact with me, she said she thought, "I was Italian or European," and that, "she never would have talked to me if she had known I was a Gringo."

My first sign of hubris which led to the fall:

I thought I was: A) different from other "gringos" and B) able to assist Soledad in her personal development. I was wrong on both counts. Hubris.

I left that bar without meeting the wife of my children. I was opening the back door of my taxi when my life changed forever. Pablo tapped me on the shoulder; I turned to see him and Soledad.

This is the starting point for Sean and Ted and Elizabeth. Life can change in an instant, and that tap on my shoulder changed the world.

He said, "This is my friend Soledad."

I replied, "Hi, Soledad, My name is John Murphy. What are you two doing right now?"

They said they were going to another bar and I said I'd join them. We went to a couple of bars and I spoke some poor Spanish and danced even poorer. When Soledad dropped me off that night I asked her what she was doing the following day. She said she was going to the beach and I told her I would meet her there. One kiss goodnight (sans tongue) and I left, knowing that I would find this beauty on the beach the following day.

Soledad doubted I could find her on the tourist packed beach but I did. We talked and took a few photos. Soledad had a fake tattoo and a fake book to read. That was about the only book she even claimed to read in the 7 years we were together. Soledad watches TV.

We later joked about how she used the tattoo and the book to "hook" me. I still have two of those photos from the day I met my children's mother.

I was thinking of this moment when Pablo tapped me on the shoulder, my own shoulders aching from supporting my rucksack as I passed Las Nubes, the school where I taught when I met my wife.

Chapter 6: Hail Mary.

The plan for the first day was simple but in no way easy: walk to Orotina and find a cheap hotel for the night. I had no idea how long it would take but I was walking for my children and with my children, so I didn't care. I could finally express what I was willing to do to see Sean, Ted and Elizabeth.

The topography of the first days walk looked like this: cross over two mountains and then walk the long straight blacktopped coastal plain. By 1pm, I made it over the first mountain and stopped to check my feet. I was discouraged and frightened; I had walked three hours but was still only a 15 minute car ride from Jaco. I was nowhere after three hours in the sun. My running shoes had already broken skin on my little toes. I sat in a deep culvert along the curve of the road and changed my shoes to a pair of old, second hand cross training mountain shoes with a hard sole. I had never walked such a distance before and was concerned about the state of my feet. I had gotten nowhere but had sustained my first injury.

"Hail Mary full of grace, the Lord is with you. Blessed are thou among women and blessed is the fruit of thy womb, Jesus. Holy Mary, mother of God, pray for us sinners, now and at the hour of our death. Amen."

I walked and prayed. It was July and I had not seen my children since the previous November when they left for Spain with Soledad. I prayed as a form of meditation. I had been introduced to prayerful meditation at age sixteen when I read <u>Franny and Zoey</u> (Salinger, 1961) which spoke of <u>The Way of the Pilgrim</u> (translated by Reginald Michael French, 1884). I clung to prayerful meditation as an emotional life raft by saying the "Hail Mary," thousands and thousands of times over.

This journey was an expression of pain. I said my prayers as a positive form of mental escapism. In a sense, I abused the prayers and meditation to distract my mind, to get out of my own troubled thoughts. I prayed and still pray the moment my mind awakes from sleep. My first thought is prayer and I start with "Hail Mary's." I say the, "Hail Mary" in English and Spanish, in case Mary is not bilingual.

"Dios te salve María, llena eres de gracia, El Señor esta contigo…"

I love the idea of praying to a woman and for better or worse, I have been worshipping women my whole life. I say four "Hail Mary's," in the morning and at night: One for each of my children and one for my wife. I am three years into this last before sleep and first to awake habit.

The theory is that through constant internal prayer our heartbeat will pump to the rhythm. In Greek the term is, "hesychasm." I had washed myself, using prayer like Clorox, to bleach the pain of life-without-my-children. Any moment when the tears came, I prayed: in the car, in the shower and now, walking 100 miles in the moccasins of a lonely estranged father wearing the countenance of a pilgrim.

I made it over the hump of one mountain and was four hours into my walk. The average walking speed is about 3 miles an hour. Between prayers and pain I did mental math on how far I had come and how much further I had to go. I stopped at a "soda" (a small restaurant), after the crest of the winding mountain road. I was four hours into the pain and rapidly dehydrating. I drank five glasses of water and a pineapple juice.

I felt different after four hours of walking: I was now a pilgrim on a mission and less a tourist on a walk. I felt more powerful than just a few hours before. I didn't know how or when I would make it to Orotina but there was a lightness of being, a higher purpose that walked beside me. The backpack that hurt after three hundred yards was now a part of me that begged no pain.

"Lord Jesus Christ, have mercy on my soul."

After the first mountain, the winding road dips down to the sea at Bill and Laura's Restaurant where an Australian man has collected antiques and made a restaurant around the rusty junk. I plodded to the sea-side of the road, laid my weary bones under a tree and slept for 20 minutes until my eyes snapped open and my mind began...

"Dios te salve María, llena eres de gracia..."

I woke up praying and sore. The next phase of the journey was a long hot coastal plain of shadeless two lane blacktop. The road runs low and straight for a distance of ten minutes by car or an hour walking. I saw a flock of scarlet macaws, counted their odd number and thought of the lonely single. Macaws are one of the few breeds that mate for life, without fail and without lawyers. They stick together and if torn apart, they never mate again. When a bird poacher steals a mated macaw they take more than one bird; they kill the line. Uneven flocks of Macaws may include one dead end gene pool. I prayed and sweated and watched the road ahead, shimmering black and wavy in the heat. A murder of crows passed noisily while silly, floppy eared Brahman cows mooed in the distance.

My feet burned from the blacktop; the air was heavy from the lowland swamp to my left. Sweat drenched my shirt, and then my paint splattered cut-off khakis until a steady trickle dripped from the hem and sizzled on the roadway. I arrived at the Crocodile Bridge, a popular tourist stop on the coastal road, that spans the Tarcoles River where a float of crocodiles, some sixteen, eighteen feet long, rest in the mud, their mouths open wide with white egrets piggybacking, picking off the parasites.

The crocks floated in midstream, mouths agape, filtering for fish to augment the influx of raw chicken that rains from the tourists. The bridge is noticeably missing many protective railings. Thieves steal the eight foot long, four inch diameter aluminum guard rails to sell for scrap. I first noticed the bent rails and tried to imagine how a car accident would bend the rail into the letter "v." The criminal recyclers bend the rail until they are able to carrying it off to sell for a few dollars.

The walkway is 18" wide and one step-up from the white line of the roadway, so no guardrail makes this brush with nature all the more exciting for the tourists: heavyset septuagenarian adventurers with unenthusiastic overweight diabetic wives; adolescent girls openly scoffing at parents from the shame of being demeaned to such activities; loud little boys, un-yet medicated and reckless, are followed by nervous overprotective mothers.

Notice the "v -shaped" bent rail to the right.

On the far side of the bridge a restaurant sells coconuts and beach towels, hammocks and fake wooden indigenous carvings done by fake indigenous artists. I stopped for protein and liquid. My journey was in its infancy but my aura changed. I was detaching from everyday life, a drawn out process, like slow Band-Aid removal. Each footfall carried me further away from my bed and closer towards my epiphany on this call to adventure. The wee stages of any adventure are beset with trials and pitfalls.

I chatted with two fresh-faced policemen in pressed uniforms who drew confidence from being armed in a country where there is mostly peace. It is a different look from the wide-eyed, clean shaven fear of Columbian police or the bored, vapid-faced Bedouins, enduring forced military service, slouching on the street corners of Cairo.

"How far is Orotina from here?" I asked.

"Only about 20 minutes," they replied.

"Muchisimas gracias," I said with a pilgrim's sincerity.

"Dios le bendiga. Que le vaya bien." "May God bless you and may your journey go well," they said to me.

I moved forward with the mental math of twenty minutes by car at 55 miles an hour and then converted that to kilometers and realized I would not get to Orotina until well after sunset. I didn't relish walking in the dark but such is the way of the pilgrim.

Chapter 7: The Law of Crece, Come.

A golden sun lowered into the Pacific. Walking allowed me to see what I didn't see whizzing by at fifty-five mph: growth, death and new life and my role in that perfect process. I am a "child of this universe, no less than the trees and the stars," (Desiderata).

Both edges of the winding two lane blacktop were peppered with reflectors every three feet for the length and breadth of the journey. Ticos (the slang name for people from Costa Rica – it is not offensive but unofficial) call the reflectors, "ojos de gatos" or just "gatos." This translates to "cat's eyes" or just "cats."

As evidence to how well the reflectors function is how many are missing. People hit the gatos at odd angles or slam on the brakes and the gatos become dislodged and broken, unhinged and scattered by the side of the road. As I measured my paces by gatos, I thought about the cars that ran them over and the distinct possibility of getting run over by a car, bus or truck.

Not much of a shoulder on this typical stretch of road.

Central Pacific Costa Rica is a subtropical climate with only two seasons: rainy and rainy as hell. Rain starts forming in the morning as the sun bakes fog from low lying areas into rising mist along the mountain sides. By the afternoon, all that moisture falls heavy and long. Samoan sized raindrops pound, like getting hit in the head with a textbook by a nun, but it is the duration of the beating which elicits both fear and admiration.

Rain falls for hours, thumping, like a Florida rain at 3pm in the summer, except this rain is that rain on meth, continuing without pause. The tricky part of road construction in Costa Rica is how to accommodate all this water. How do we move it where we want it to go?

Concrete culverts along the sides of winding mountain roads are eight feet deep and six feet wide. I was walking on the one foot wide shoulder between the culvert on my left and the vehicles on my right that are filled with city folk drinking in preparation for their beach holiday or young kids texting while driving their parents' car. Families packed into mini-vans with kids distracting dad and tiny Tica soccer moms sitting on phone books guide their 8 cylinder SUV's while tractor trailer drivers, awake for fifteen hours, juiced on caffeine and Peruvian Marching powder, all fly by within inches of me on the tight curves.

"Hail Mary full of grace, the lord is with thee…"

This was not a pilgrimage on a sidewalk. Those mothers of children in Jaco had the right idea. With my feet burning and the sun falling closer to the horizon I considered giving-up. It was too dangerous to walk along the road in Costa Rica. I could get killed and what good would that do my children?

I had walked for seven hours and had found my excuse: This was too dangerous. So I gave up, and felt relieved by that decision. The bus wasn't passing me at the time, so I kept on walking for lack of a better alternative. I was a pilgrim by default.

"Jesus Christ, Lord have mercy on my soul."

Having lived in Costa Rica for a total of four years, I am now never surprised at what people eat. There is a theory called, "The Law of Crece, Come." It translates to, "if it grows, eat it." People eat all kinds of wild looking fruits and vegetables and plants and roots. Ugly things that you imagine the first person, who took a bite, did so only on a dare.

"Mammones," are as big as a man's thumb with soft spines and insides like eyeballs. They are slimy and sweet with a nut core.

They run about a dollar a pound unless, you are a tourist, and then they are two dollars a pound, but tourists don't eat these things. They are too scary looking for the uninitiated, but Costa Ricans love them and I enjoyed them as well. Apart from eating them, Costa Ricans love throwing the skins out the window of their cars. I had walked for seven hours along the road and I swear I never went more than 50 feet without seeing the skin of a mammon.

I arrived at another "soda." This small family owned restaurant was connected to a house with a few benches that overlooked the Nicoya Gulf and the city of Puntarenas, where Eduardo (my children's great grandfather) had begun his walk some 80 years before. Our elevation was about 2,000 feet, the green jungle ran recklessly down the mountain to meet blue water, then further on, sea met sky along a razor wire horizon while the now orange sun dipped slowly into the water, like a bather easing into a chilly pool.

Since I was walking, the family who owned the soda and I went through the round of questions: "Where was I from? Where did I start my journey and why was I walking?"

In Spanish, the word for why people walk is a, "Prometa." It looks like the word "promise" and it means the same. What promise had I asked of the Virgin in exchange for my devotion to her on this walk? I told them I was walking so I could see my children who were separated from me by my wife. They shook their heads in a knowing way. Mothers taking their children away from fathers are common in Costa Rica.

It started with bad apples on both sides. Father's ran away and the personal reaction is that mothers believe that children don't need fathers. After generations of the same, the predominant belief has grown into an acceptable cultural reality. In Costa Rica, there is a predominant belief that children don't need their fathers, they just need money.

I wish I was making that up, but I was living it.

I asked how far it was to Orotina and a clean cowboy rancher, a man in his middle forties who had the ease of financial security with his late model Toyota Hilux and pressed Wrangler jeans told me, "Only about 15 minutes." I did the mental math and was looking at about another 3 hours of walking.

He offered me a ride to Orotina and I was tempted for a moment but I had made my promise to the Virgin, so I continued walking. There is no hitchhiking on the road to redemption.

"Dios te salve María, llena eres de gracia…"

I passed a six foot long black snake that had been pounded flat into the asphalt. It was 6pm and I had been on the road for 8 hours as I approached the toll booths for the highway to Orotina. I was so excited to see a sign with a picture of a person walking and a red "X" over the person: "No Peatones." "No walkers." I could see the sign from a hundred meters away and was hoping this would be the end of my journey. Please tell me to stop this foolishness. All I needed was an excuse.

When I arrived at the toll booth the smiling uniformed attendant waved me on. "Damn," I thought. I asked if I could pass, hoping he would change his mind and we would obey the law but this was the time of the pilgrims so he happily waved me on. I suffered a moment of disappointment but continued on just the same; the maxim of the Brute Irish ringing in my soul: just try harder.

Chapter 8: Children Don't Need a Father.

The muscles in my legs cramped down hard on themselves in the darkness and although the sign said it was three kilometers to Orotina, I still had about an hour to walk and then find a place to lay my weary bones.

I hobbled across the dark highway to an open air bus stop shelter with no walls, a roof and a metal bench. I lay on the ground and put my feet up on the bench and rested. I thought of my journey thus far. It was 8pm and I had been on the march for about ten hours and still had miles to go before I slept.

Where are my children and where do they think I am? My mind clicked away from those thoughts:

"Hail Mary full of grace, the Lord is with you, blessed art thou among women..."

After two years of celibate faithfulness to my wife, when I arrived in Costa Rica, I kept my wedding ring on. When I was served with the Restraining Order and was certain that my wife would not reconcile nor allow me to see or speak with my children, I took my wedding ring off.

This was July 2011. The first Costa Rican woman with whom I shared my story told me this, "Children do not need a father." She was serious, not harboring hate or trying to hurt me. She believed that to the core of her being, it was ingrained in her culture and I was a fool to believe otherwise.

She had also been a single mother. She put a restraining order on her husband and he was never allowed to see the children and he eventually gave up. I wasn't ever going to give up and become a deadbeat dad. Not me. Not possible.

The second woman I dated was a single mother. She allowed her ex to see the children but she too had put a restraining order on him shortly after the birth of her their child. She said he was controlling with an anger problem. She said he never hit her. This pattern was scaring the hell out of me.

I had only dated two women and both told me the story of my wife.

Is this culture?

Then my third and the fourth female lovers told me the same.

I didn't know just how many women in Costa Rica believe that children don't need a father. I didn't know Soledad believed that. Either I never asked specifically or she just never let me know her deepest beliefs, either way, we have all paid heavily for the one philosophical misconnect between my wife and me.

I now know that the children belong to the mother. Children belong to the mother. That is a universal truth. Fathers and philosophers can believe otherwise but what stands as truth in theory, fathers and mothers have equal rights, is false in practice.

No one, ever again, can convince me otherwise.

"Dios te salve María, llena eres de gracia..."

I picked myself way up off the ground and moved forward with my pilgrimage, in the dark, along a lonely road to Orotina for the night.

I scanned the fresh blacktop with a small Maglite in a continuous arc in front of me. I thought of that six foot black snake I saw smashed into the pavement two hours ago. There were no streetlights and a shallow moon offered me little hope of seeing snakes in the dark. Snakes enjoy the heat from the blacktop as night falls. They slip across and aren't looking out for us. We have to look out for them.

The daylight dangers of cars and trucks and buses was no less real, in fact, the getting hit by a bus scenario increased with nightfall but now the stepping on a snake scenario just became a real pain in the ass.

"Hail Mary, full of grace the Lord is with you....Jesus Christ Lord have mercy on my soul."

At 9pm, I was eleven hours into this walk. My mind and body were numb but I could not yet bring myself to sleep on the ground again. I stopped at the two-room Police Station of Orotina and waited for the older Sergeant with the cheap moustache and doughy mid-section to finish with his personal phone call. Maybe he thought I couldn't speak Spanish or he just didn't care, but I stood for five minutes until he was good and ready to end his conversation. He wasn't cursed with self-awareness or an achy need to serve.

I asked if there was a hostel or cheap hotel and he pointed me north towards the square without really giving me any definite answer or directions. "Pa' alla…" "That way."

The square of Orotina is a traditional colonial plaza with the park in the center, the Church on the north side and shops and markets surrounding. There are high shade oaks covering the square with concrete benches where old folk flattened their bottoms playing checkers and young folk sit real close and kiss until their blood rushes up. On this night there were food stands, games, children, parents, music and dancing in the night. It was a celebration honoring the Patron Saint of Costa Rica – The Virgin of the Angels, which welcomed me with open arms to Orotina.

"Hail Mary full of grace, the Lord is with you…"

I wandered down a side street and asked a group of half-drunk 20 something's if they knew of any hotels. They pointed down the street and told me the name. This pilgrim needed to eat, shower and lie down.

I found El Gallo (The Cock) Motel and bought half a roasted chicken on the way. I was exhausted, a mess and beyond all but minimum communication. The girl at the front desk eyed me with suspicion but since I had money and my passport, she gave me a room.

I was physically hobbled, no longer walking, more like limping along, crusty with road grime and sweat. I ate that chicken with unclean hands like an animal (except with hands), solely to avoid making two trips to the bathroom.

I had never before walked 11 hours; the only training I had was eating Philadelphia Cheese Steaks on a regular basis.

My feet were a shame; I didn't even want to look. It was impossible for my body to bend, so I shook my shorts and underwear to the bathroom floor.

I stood under hot water for half an hour, soaping away but still felt unclean from the dust and smog that had permeated my skin.

I texted my friend Jose, informing him that I had arrived in Orotina alive.

I thought of where Sean and Ted and Elizabeth were sleeping and how their distance from me can only be measured in miles. I thought of our bedtime ritual together and how getting into our pajamas had become a triumph on the road to empowerment. I remember it this way:

Pajama Time

Sean and Ted were five and three at the time. We lived in our two bedroom single home in Bensalem with their smaller bedroom caddy corner to our modest sized bedroom. On their white door hung two wooden signs, hand painted with the names Sean Patrick and Theodore Joseph. I still have those signs after years of not seeing my sons. Sean's has a picture of an elephant and Ted's has a picture of a bear.

I painted their bedroom walls light blue and dark blue carpet covered the floor. Two double sashed wooden windows on opposing walls trapped the closet at the corner. The 50 year old aluminum Venetian blinds still functioned well from lack of ever being moved. They splintered the sunlight that entered in the morning. I took black and white pictures with a Nikon F SRL camera. I have an original with me now, Sean is looking up at me, head tilted, squinting and smiling, his face diagonally corrugated by rows of shade and slivers of blinding white sunlight.

Sean had a blue racecar bed and Ted had graduated into an orange and blue metal frame bed with a construction worker theme. A black skull and crossbones flag hung from a hook and was countered by a larger U.S. flag. (Right now that Pirate flag flutters in the breeze outside my home in Mexico. It stands as a symbol of my rebellion and subsequent exile from Costa Rica.) Two small light houses rested on a yellow shelf and a picture of a spooners moon smiled down.

Our favorite books were: Dr. Seuss, Goodnight Moon and illustrated books on Transportation and Dinosaurs. We read almost every night until Green Eggs and Ham was memorized. The books were neatly stacked next to the Thomas the Train child size futon that folds out into a bed. We passed hours and films and naps and snacks on that futon.

Pajamas signify the end of the day, the party is almost over and "lights out" confinement will begin promptly, like a low security prison for children. We confine our children to bed while adults flaunt freedom. I don't wonder why children rebel and escape. I know I don't like being forced and trapped. Nobody does. I too, have a natural resistance to closure. Pajama time can be an hour long process with shouts and tears but we outsmarted this resistance culture and found power in the pajama ritual.

Many psychologists suggest using a timer to encourage children to accomplish a goal. A definitive end time (e.g. three minutes) to accomplish a task only adds pressure and marks a definitive line of failure. Counting-up (i.e. starting at zero) marks the success upon completion of task. Count up for success.

The boys stood naked in the living room, fresh from the shower and giggling with anticipation, pajamas in hand. "Ready. Set. Go." At random intervals I called out official time, "Twenty seconds on my mark. Aaaand Mark." With total concentration they flopped to the floor to slip legs in trouser holes, and then rolled back to shoulder blades to pass the waistband over buttocks. The top was a crap shoot with buttons. Sometimes I helped Ted with the buttons and on lucky nights it was a pullover without buttons. Ted was just three and a half at the time and learning early and holding his own. He was budding into digital and manual dexterity and way ahead of the curve.

The first night it took less than 5 minutes to be in full bedtime uniform with the head cleared of all the days' dirty clothes. On hands and knees with backsides in the air, the boys pushed the clothes bulldozer-style down the laundry chute.

The first night we floated on high fives, drunk on endorphins and success. Success becomes addictive once the neural paths to that feeling are established. Allowing children to find success with all its residual benefits is a basic goal in education for learners at any level.

The next night we did the same. The boys shaved off more time for the Pajama Putting World Record but that was of little importance. The larger picture was that they were big boys who could dress themselves and the 40 minute pajama ritual of shouts and cries was over. We Tai Chi'd a possibly negative experience into a full form positive empowering exercise.

Soledad came into the room when we finished that first night. She smiled wide, titled her head like she does and glowed with pride. The boys had tasted empowerment and they liked the flavor.

Within a week or so, quickly undressing and dressing was routine and we moved on to bicycles, carpentry, swimming, and handwriting.

"Hail Mary full of grace....Lord Jesus Christ have mercy on my soul."

Four times I say that, then sleep.

Chapter 9: Dog Whisperer.

Day Two:

Orotina to La Garita

6am-9pm

15 hours

Eyes open. Pain.

"Dios te salve María, llena eres de gracias…Lord Jesus Christ, please help Sean."

And then one for Ted and Elizabeth and my wife.

It is 5:30am and although I should sleep some more, today's journey will be far more challenging that the previous. This day I will go up and over the mountains.

"El Aguacate," *the road over the mountains.*

I am hobbled like a Bedouin camel, limping on constricted muscles. It will take me another day to learn to stretch like mad. So for now, I limp over to the office to drop off the room key. The sun is up and ready to test me today.

I have a decision to make. There is a new highway that will cut both the distance and difficulty from my trip. The problem is that there are no convenient New Jersey Turnpike-like rest stops where I can veer off and buy a Gatorade.

The other option is over the old highway called, "El Aguacate." It is an equally desolate venture but does provide some roadside stops that will offer food and drink. This road will also take more time and more effort and is more dangerous because of the fog and the curves and non-existent shoulder.

I consult the two men in the office who are sitting down for their morning cup a' joe. I answer their questions about my journey. They are empathetic. The pilgrimage is a cultural norm. It is the only viable form of expression available to me to demonstrate my commitment…my love…my grit. (Yeah, I'm gritty alright. That and fifty cents will get me a cup of coffee.)

The old boys agree that El Aguacate will provide a better opportunity to find water, so with a tip of my hat and "Dios les Bendiga," I am a pilgrim on the second day of my walk. The unknowing grabs me in a moment of respite: What are my children doing right now? Are they watching cartoons in their pajamas, smelling of sleep?

"Dios Te salve María, llena eres de gracia."

Orotina was a stop on the railroad from Coastal Puntarenas to the central valley capital city of San Jose. The railroad is now defunct but the remembrance of times past still lie in parallel lines dissecting the quaint town.

I thought of Abuelo, Soledad´s grandfather. He was born in 1918 and he passed these exact railroad lines that I am passing now, on his way to San Jose as a young barefooted orphan.

The next town on the way to San Jose is San Mateo (Saint Matthew). It is a smaller version of Orotina with a central park, large trees, and cement benches where the old sit and the young play, but at 6:30am on a Sunday, the park was silent and empty.

The houses of San Mateo are small wooden rectangles. Tiny porches and tiny gardens where tires and empty buckets act as planters for the flowers that grow at will. The dark earth of Costa Rica and the elevated cool climate make growing anything easy. Spit a papaya seed and in six weeks you will have a papaya tree in the front yard.

As I rounded through San Mateo, I had to cross three bridges above noisy creeks. It was green and cool at 7:30 in the morning and the houses became less frequent as the road stretched and winded up the mountain.

A newer house on my right was set back from the road with the dogs out front: unleashed and unfettered, the little black and white mutt with pointy nose and pointy ears, came charging at me, barking and threatening, while what looked to be Boxer-Mastiff mix, a big thick-muscled slobbery dog, was lumbering my way as well. Napoleon (I had already named him) was at me, snapping and barking, I wasn't as worried about him as I was the potential damage the 90lb hulk could inflict.

This could end bloody.

Chapter 10: Dangerous Roads.

This little dog in front of me outside San Mateo was my one conflict with wildlife. He was looking to take a bite if I turned my back. I wished I had a stick, realizing too late why so many of the pilgrims carry walking sticks. My life was funny like that.

I bent down slowly to pick-up a fallen branch long enough to keep this little guy at bay. Fortunately, the big dog just stood back and watched the show; deciding not to get involved just yet.

The rotted limb with which I was holding off Napoleon broke in half after I rapped him once on his pointy nose. Again, I found myself holding the short end of the stick.

I slowly backed myself up the road and found another stick that had not yet yielded to the fecund rot of the rain forest.

After a hundred yards Napoleon stopped and I waved good-bye. He was a good mutt. He performed his duty like a pro, like the Swiss for the Pope. I now had a decent walking stick and was looking to trade-up for one that better suited me.

I started anew: *"Hail Mary, full of grace the Lord is with you..."*

San Geronimo is a small town by any standards. There is one small pulperia (small family owned convenience store). They have one bar, one diner, a small church and a soccer pitch. I stopped at the open air diner to push down some protein for a day that I knew would be endlessly long.

I ate the traditional fried eggs and gallo pinto (rice and beans). The food was greasy but the toast helped. I was still hobbling but I would get used to this leg cramped walking over the next 12 hours. Pain is a part of this life and a part of this walk. I would walk through the pain.

I went outside the diner and lay on the ground to sleep for a few minutes. It was 8:30am and the sun was rising strong in the sky. I slept for about 20 minutes and my eyes jumped open.

Pain. Where the hell am I?

"Dios te salve María, llena eres de gracia....Jesus Christ, Lord have mercy on my soul."

I got to my knees first, then pushed myself to a standing position and carried on.

Like most miles I had walked before, and the many miles ahead, there was no shoulder on this winding, steeply inclined stretch of road. This part of the road is where chunky tow trucks, 70's Toyota Land Cruisers, geared low for the steep climb, idly sit roadside, waiting for cars to over-heat. Every day and every night cars just can't handle the climb and they die out.

I wondered if *I* was ready for the steep curvy climb.

I pushed-on without a shoulder to walk on (or cry on), and a large open trench to my left. The curves were particularly dangerous. I approached each bend and listened for the sound of motors barreling down the road, then made a break for it. There is little room for error on the curves. Several scary times I was caught on a curve, standing still, looking into the face of an equally startled driver, our eyes acknowledging that we were playing with life as they passed with only inches to spare.

"Dios te salve María, llena eres de gracias..."

What else could I do but pray?

I thought of my children. I thought of our time together and I remembered the glory. I valued the moments of goodness, when we rode bikes together on streets with wide sidewalks and traffic lights.

I thought of the bike ride when Sean saw angels.

Sean Sees Angels

Sean whispered, "Papá, there are angels in those chairs."

Katherine Drexel was richer than rich in the 1920's, at a $1,000 a day, her trust fund ranneth over, but instead of living a carefree socialite existence in Philadelphia, after a conversation with the Pope, she decided to devote her life to the Catholic Church and most specifically to Blacks and Indians (or African Americans and Native Americans if you'll have it that way).

She has since been canonized a Saint. One of her three miracles was curing the Gutherman boy in 1974, who was by all accounts deaf until the long dead Katharine Drexel (then known as Mother Katharine Drexel) got involved.

She started her own brand of nuns, known as the Sisters of the Blessed Sacrament. She built her mother house in Bensalem, just outside of Philadelphia. It is a sprawling Italian Renaissance stone affair with curved verandas and infinite columns supporting the clay tile roof. The stone masons who built the place knew their work. It is a lump of stone and cement that will never fall down.

The Chapel is all dark shiny wood that creaks, with painted frescos that sigh and stained glass that winks. The beauty and sanctity is profound. Chapels are poems compared to epic cathedrals; it takes discerning skill to distill beauty into a confined space.

Mother Katharine's chapel is rounded and narrow like a drum. On opposite walls are carved wooden chairs with intricate filigreed and dark wood that is shiny from the backsides of the blessed sisters. The chairs are raised from the floor level and could accommodate a Samoan but find happiness with the thin nuns.

There aren't many of the sisters left these days; they are on the Endangered Species list of Catholic Institutions. The church has really taken a hit on women willing to donate their lives to Christ. There are only 113 left and many are in the later years of their life and waiting to meet Christ and Mother Katherine in the Chapel.

The mother house sits on 50 acres that is just two blocks from my parents' house in Bensalem. Sean, Ted and I rode our bicycles there the summer before my wife took our children to Costa Rica and I stayed in the U.S. to support us. That was the last summer we had together.

My parents, Pop and Grandma to my children, live about 2 miles from our house, which doesn't sound like much, except if you are 4 and 6 years old and travelling by bicycle. It was a full adventure to arrive at Pop's and we were spent for the rest of the day. We didn't even ride the bikes home. We threw them in the back of Pop's white Mazda pick-up truck.

We set out at 9am before the sun got too high and too hot. The four block ride to the end of our neighborhood brought us to our first crossing of a major street: Route 13, Bristol Pike. We crossed at the traffic light and passed the manicured lawn of Fleur Funeral Home: a stone and column box that exudes calm and somber times like good funeral homes should.

Passing down through the Poquessing neighborhood we passed skinny Victorians in brick and iron rail then crossed through Andalusia Schoolyard Playground. I went to that Kindergarten when I was 5. "The more we change, the more we stay the same," I thought. I had traveled through 19 countries and learned three languages only to come back to my kindergarten playground with my two young sons.

Pop's store was on the corner, 25 yards from the entrance of Andalusia Schoolyard. Murphy's Budget Bakery was housed in a three bay garage block building with the store front facing Route 13. My parents spent 13 years in that building, open six days a week, from 7am until 7pm, when the lottery number was picked.

My mom came home at 6 or so to fix supper for when Pop finished at the store. I don't think my parents closed it for more than Sundays and two hands full of Saturdays in all those 13 years. I never saw a vacation that lasted more than two days. For "vacations" we would leave on a Friday night and return Sunday night. That is the life of the small business owner and his children.

Murphy's Budget Bakery (they never really baked anything) is now a small windowed, check cashing place that sells cigarettes and Zippos. The lottery machine is still there but nowadays there is a lottery machine in every shop and supermarket, so they don't make the money that Pop did. Pop got out when the getting was good.

We snaked behind the store to pass through the gravel parking lot of the VFW. A large stone three story Victorian with two imposing black anchors and an American Flag out front and cigarette smoking vets drinking cheap beer and shots in the back. My Uncle Jimmy used to get his fix there. They give out hot dogs on Memorial Day when everybody thinks it is ok to get drunk in the morning.

There is sidewalk for the next two blocks until we reached Carla's Waterice, where Aunt Joanne worked for 25 years from scooper to Director of Operations until the franchise grew to 100 stores. She is a model of business smarts and hard work.

We passed by the waterice stand and moved north on Bristol Pike passing in front of Woodhaven Mall, where I took Sean on his first "date" with his first "girlfriend", Alexa, a blond girl that Sean said he loved. He was five.

We rode on the sidewalk of the Woodhaven Road overpass. We watched the cars zoom by below and felt the gentle tremble of the concrete bridge. I told the boys what Uncle Mike told me, "If the bridge didn't shake it would crack." We appreciated the logic but were still unnerved by the shaky bridge. After the bridge, we made a right turn before the dangerous parking lot of the busiest Wawa in the chain.

The small street behind Wawa crosses onto the back entrance of Mother Katharine's estate and shrine. Entering from the back we rode up the hill to the service entrance. We parked the bikes and walked quietly past the noisy pond and faced the carved oak, iron-hung doors to enter into the side of the chapel.

The narrowness of the chapel reminded me of the saying that relates to the size of homes, "The smaller a home, the easier it is to fill with love." The same holds true for Chapels. We stepped from the bright day into dim light and heavy silence.

We sat at mid-chapel; the mood of the space dictated our behavior. I didn't have to say anything about being quiet. On either side of the chapel are the individual carved thrones where the sisters have sat and prayed and dozed for more than a 100 years.

We sat in silence, my sons' legs dangling and mine firm on the floor when Sean leaned into me and whispered, "Papá, there are angels in those chairs." There is my son the seer, attuned to the vibrations of spirits and reverent to their energy.

"Yes, Sean, there are angels in those chairs."

It wasn't a miracle to Sean and Ted paid the comment no mind, but I was witness to the heartstrings of Sean and his sense of things not seen. It had happened before in his life: the time he saw and spoke with a long since dead Edward Robbins, his memory of his baptism when he was only two and a half, and although unconscious, his brief ride in the ambulance in NYC after three hours of surgery.

We left the chapel, cruised up the tree lined entrance and exited through massive wrought iron gates flanked by stone walls. Crossing the street, we had only to drift two blocks downhill to arrive at Pop's house.

Grandma greeted us with drinks and so went our longest adventure yet. The boys' world was expanding. I have not been with my children for over four years now, but I know that during our time together I instilled a sense of wonder.

Even though I am not with them, their distance from me can only be measured in miles. Their limits and vision are not bound to this world because they see angels where others see only empty chairs.

Chapter 11: Empower the Children with Responsibility.

In 2005, Soledad, Sean and I lived in the house next to my mother-in-law's house in La Uruca, San Jose, Costa Rica. The three bedroom house had a small enclosed garden off the living room and a large upstairs master bedroom with thin carpet. Every morning when Sean was a year and a half old, he woke up with the sun at 5am.

Every morning I woke up at 5am with Sean. I brought him into our bedroom and we played on the floor and watched, "Finding Nemo." Still both sleepy-eyed and half-awake, we lay on the floor amid a cloud of blankets and pillows and started the film that started our day together.

What I love most about this film is the mythology. This film is based on the "Journey of the Hero," as explained by Joseph Campbell. We are all heroes and we are all on a journey in this life. The question arises: What will you do with your journey?

A character that stands out in the film "Finding Nemo," is Crush. He is the sea turtle father. At one point his offspring, "Squirt," is pushed out of the current. Marlin immediately panics but Crush places a fin on Marlin's shoulder to stop him and says. "Kill the motor dude. Let's see what Offspring can do on his own."

Crushes' quote sums up my fathering style. I allowed my children to experience life and sometimes life bit back. Just like Crush knew that the experience of falling out of the current was dangerous but that Squirt could handle it. Squirt comes back pumped up and confident. Squirt is empowered and that was my goal with my children. Empower the children is my mantra.

So many parents over-protect by bubble wrapping their children in hope of "saving" them from pain and danger. The result is children who are weak and useless. I am not saying that allowing a child to drive a car on the highway at age ten is a good idea. I don't recommend it, but sitting your child on your lap, on a back road or empty parking lot and allowing them to feel the control of the car is an empowering experience. How many farmers kids (when there were farmers) grew up on their daddy's lap feeling the power of a John Deere tractor beneath their hands.

I did the same with all the tools I used. My children have used an electric drill and electric saw. They felt the dangerous cutting power in the safety of my hands over their hands. We took away all the curiosity and mystery that surrounds dangerous machines. My children had felt the power and respected the tool.

Ted and Sean were 3 and 5 when we started working in the garden in Bensalem. We used small hand shovels to dig out the weeds. When the soil was small, pebbly and loose, I stood up and dropped the 8 inch metal hand shovel face-down into the soil and it stuck.

We loved the perfection of the sound as metal slipped past soil line and dug in. Shoomp! There is a satisfaction and an understanding of the physical forces of gravity and weight and balance. We played with the hand shovels, dropping them into the soil so they stuck and then graduated to giving screw drivers a one rotation toss before they stuck into the muddy ground with satisfaction.

Over the course of months, dropping and sticking and one rotation sticks lead to a cardboard box with a bull's eye. We said, "Ready on the left, ready on the right, ready on the firing line. All clear. Fire!"

It was supervised and under control until someone like Marlin showed-up.

In one corner of the yard, our pond is backed-up to the fence and the white shed. A well-trimmed shade tree that started out as a weed was in the center of old raspberry bushes that have not yielded fruit since I was a boy and I should know because I grew up in the house next door.

When we arrived from Costa Rica in 2007, that corner of the property was overgrown and lost. Every week I rammed the lawn mower deeper into the stickers and after a month, the stickers and the weeds were down to only a few thick stalks. I found a Pinky

Ball that I lost in those bushes 25 years beforehand. I lost it the day I bought it, which is probably why I remember it so well. That ball flew off the wooden bat, over the fence and into the middle of those sticker bushes. I thought it was gone forever.

After a quarter century lying in the underbrush, the ball all but fell apart in my 37 year old hands, but I found it, just like I'll find my children.

I dug our pond and made a waterfall under the shade of the small tree. I pruned any branch that was pointing down until the whole tree leapt towards the sun. I supported a 2" x 8" board across some branches with rope and the boys started climbing. There is an old sailors saying that I taught my boys about climbing, "One hand for the ship and one hand for yourself."

Climbing is an empowerment exercise and the boys loved it. Sean sat on the board and had a whistle hanging off of a broken branch. He said he was the lifeguard.

I saw how empowered and confident the boys were when we met for our supervised visits in the court house in 2012 in San Jose, Costa Rica. It was during our family meeting that Sean asked, "When can we see you again?"

I said, "I don't know. It is not up to me, we have to wait to see what the judge says. The judge will make a decision."

Teddyboy jumped up, "Where is the judge? I want to talk with the judge to tell her I want to go with you."

Sean spoke up, "Yeah, I want to talk with the judge too. I want to swim in your pool."

Empowered little men. Teddyboy acted instantly in a Zen moment without thought, only pure action, like Bruce Lee playing Ping-Pong.

My children inspire me. They have grit, passion and intelligence. They continue on without me, on their own journey, with the confidence of dragon slayers. Sean and Ted showed their mettle in a dingy room in the courthouse.

Chapter 12: Restaurants.

"El Aguacate" is the road over the mountains that leads to Alajuela, which for me, on this second day of my peregrination, is the Promised Land. I thought I could find a cheap hotel somewhere near Alajuela. I wasn't too concerned because looking for that hotel was still 8 hours away.

Mountain road building and downhill skiing are based on the same concept: You can't go too straight for too far, because you either can't slow down or on the opposite end, make it up the hill. So the path must be curvy with switchbacks and dangerous drop-offs. The payoff for brief lapses of concentration is a scenic view during the last seconds of life. They locate those cars by following the party buzzards gliding thermals above the wreckage.

I could never see more than a hundred yards ahead because the road was steadily rising curves. At 10:30am I had been on the road for about five hours…up, up and up into the clouds. There is a restaurant with an impressive overlook of the valley below. The vista is for miles or only several feet, depending on the clouds. On this morning, from this spot, I could see the ocean, more than a day's walk behind me.

The Treehouse Bar was closed but I knocked on the door. A young fellow came out and told me they didn't open until 11am. I was spent. My feet hurt. Each step was on broken blisters worn down to bare red skin. My calves were knots. The young owner saw I wasn't leaving, so he opened the door and asked me to come inside. He was there with his staff from a party the night before. Beer bottles littered every flat surface of the 1,000 square foot restaurant. Ashtrays overflowed and the raw stink of spilled beer and spoiled hops belied the beauty of the morning mist rising along the side of the verdant mountains. The staff was having a drink, smoking and discussing the highlights of the night before, and I, a pilgrim on a journey, sat with them and smoked a butt. I lived the waiter's life for four lost years in both New York City and Boston until I began my career in education with my first teaching job in Cairo, Egypt.

Chapter 13: A Journey with Abuelo.

I had visited the Treehouse Bar some years before with Eduardo Garcia McDaniel, my children's maternal great grandfather. Eduardo (I call him Abuelo) and I took a three hour car trip to Miramar, where Abuelo had lived for four years until his mother died and he ran out of parents and became an orphan.

We left from San Jose early in the morning and he drove. Abuelo was 88 years old at the time but his enthusiasm for life was just past the drinking age. As I look back on it now, it seems strange that an 88 year old man would be driving while I rode shotgun, but that is the way Abuelo rolls.

You never really know a person until you are alone with them because group dynamics allow for social buffers. You can buffer yourself from people and remain friendly in a group for years. You want to really get to know someone? Take a car trip with them or fish alone with them at night in a small launch on the big sea. "Get to know you time," is unavoidable when two people are alone for hours in a small space trying to manage directions, food, bladder breaks and music while somehow filling the empty air with meaningful conversation or comfortable silence.

Abuelo and I set out on a bright morning and he was thrilled to be free. He is a vibrant man, hard and small with tough leather skin, a thick shock of white hair and a joke on hand. He is a young tough, will always be such and is not comfortable in the body of an old man. Ostensibly, we were looking for a beach property for me to buy, but the real journey was back in time to the places where Abuelo lived during his long life. We first stopped at an old mine close to where he lived as a boy outside of Orotina.

He told me his stories along the way and I was happy to chronicle the passage of his time on this earth although I have forgotten most of it. His great grandfather was a Scot who went to Jamaica and married a black woman. They came to Costa Rica in search of a better life, as people have done since people were alive.

He told me the story of how his great grandfather was working as a carpenter on a house of an old woman and when they took down the roof a kerchief of gold coins fell to the ground. He took that gold and went on his way.

He settled in Orotina where the train would pass the market square once a day and the people came to see what there was to see.

After Abuelo's father died, his mother moved him and his three sisters to Miramar. When she died, he was 12 and the oldest boy. He left his aunt and sisters and walked alone along the railroad tracks to San Jose to find his fortune, or at least some food and a living. He sold newspapers in the street and worked at a barber shop.

He met Abuela when she was young and they married young, as was the custom of folk in the early part of the 19th century in Costa Rica.

He had the foresight to learn about airplane engines, newfangled inventions of the times and he was positioned for the take-off of transportation by flight. It was a good time for those on the winning side of politics, for others, like Abuelo, it was time to leave. He didn't articulate and I didn't push for details. Suffice to say, he found himself on the wrong side of politics in the late 1940's and fled to Venezuela where he would live for 25 years and raise his five Costa Rican children, sending the oldest boy to Italy to become a medical doctor who would return to Costa Rica and gain some renown as a leader in the Costa Rican medical community.

After Abuelo and I visited Miramar and Bajamar, where he also spent time as a child, we visited Tivives. We found the perfect house to buy that day, 100 yards from the beach; you could hear the waves from the bedroom.

What stands out most about the day was when the car broke down at sunset outside the Treehouse Bar and Restaurant. We were blessed to break down in front of the restaurant and we sat and had coffee in the exact spot where I was sitting then, five years later. Turns-out, the gas gauge was off to begin with and we were on a steep incline, so it appeared that we had gas, but we were on empty. Abuelo, the airplane engine mechanic, figured that out. We had gas brought from Atenas, which is just a 10 minute drive up and down the mountain or a two hour walk for a pilgrim. I thought of Abuelo and his hardy good nature and decided that I would take a detour from my pilgrimage and visit him tomorrow on my way to see the Virgin. I would ask for a glass of water.

I left the sleepy, hung-over wait staff and thanked the owner for his kindness. He told me that Alajuela was about 50km from San Jose central and that most people take a bus to San Jose and then walk to see the statue of the Virgin. I wasn't most people. It would be miles to go before I slept and I began the rest of my journey with a single step.

"Holy Mary, Mother of God, pray for us sinners, now and at the hour of our death…"

Chapter 14: No Hay Nada Mas Difícil.

The higher I climbed, the more turns I took, the darker grew the skies. I had a camera with me but was always too exhausted to take off my pack and pull it out for the vistas. I thought that I could always come back and take the pictures that I missed.

I never thought that I would eventually have to escape from Costa Rica, bribing border guards and evading the police and leaving any chance of taking those pictures far behind.

I walked through clouds, tasting them as I went, while praying in earnest.

"Dear Lord, Jesus Christ, please help my children."

I arrived in Atenas and a found drug store where I bought aspirin and a Bed-Gay type muscle cream. I lathered my legs and massaged myself while I downed a Gatorade. I don't take many pills but I pushed three aspirin into my system. My legs felt better with the cream loosening the muscles and I stretched for the first time and moved on.

Many Costa Ricans work six days a week, so Sunday is the day to go to a restaurant/bar. Singles, couples and families, drink, eat and watch soccer games. It is a mirror of the U.S. football season where overweight packs of men sit half drunk, pushing fried food into their coronary arteries at great pace and yelling at images of men chasing a ball on a flat screen hung from the wall.

The more reserved of the Sunday patrons arrived in cars from church. Simple Hyundai's and pricey SUVs lined the roads and Sunday-best dressed children ate chicharones (fried pork) and fried yucca while parents sip Imperials (Costa Rican brand of beer) with ice.

Construction workers sat on stools with a battalion of dead soldiers lined up so they don't lose count with the bartender when the bill comes. Six and eight bottles stood testament to how hard these men work and drink. The jukeboxes played familiar songs.

When I first moved to Costa Rica and before I knew the mother of my children, I lived next to a cantina like the ones I passed in Atenas that day on my pilgrimage. The voice of Marc Antonio Solis blasted from the Atenas bar and it took be back to my days before I spoke Spanish.

In Jaco, in 2003, the most popular song was "No Hay Nada Mas Dificil Que Vivir Sin Ti." "There is Nothing More Difficult Than to Live Without You."

At its height, every person who entered the open air cantina was obligated to play that song; men and women looked starry eyed through brown beer bottles in hopes of finding love. The song was the Spanish version of Barry White singing, "Sexual Healing." It is a song of foreplay and because it worked, it was played at least ten times a night.

The result was that I heard that song from my bed ten times a night from the lungs of the loudest jukebox on the market. Since the chorus is repeated four times within the song, I heard the chorus words forty times per night. It is a "sticky" song by Malcolm Gladwell standards. The most frustrating part was that I didn't speak Spanish, so, "No hay nada mas dificil que vivir sin ti" became a humming "dana naana na dananaa que vivir simti." And it stuck with me for days and weeks on end, tonguing the soft pallet of my mind.

It provided the springboard to Spanish language acquisition, born of the desire to evict this song from the cheap apartment of my brain.

I learned the song and the words and more songs and more words, lots of them and all before the age of YouTube. I sat with a CD player, deciphered words and left blank lines where I knew a word existed but didn't know what that word was. I listened to Maná sing "En Muelle de San Blas" and tunes from Mercedes Sosa until I ruined the songs from overuse.

As a pilgrim born the day before, passing the 18th hour of my walk, the words of Marc Antonio penetrated my mind. There is nothing more difficult than living without you. Those were the emotions that I sought to express to Sean, Ted, Elizabeth, and to the courts and to my wife and to the lawyers who stared dry eyed and impatient when I couldn't bring myself to speak because the sobs and the tears gagged my voice.

There has been nothing more difficult that living without my children.

After almost four years I still feel like they have been kidnapped. Someone took Sean, Teddy and Elizabeth, and I am neither allowed to see or speak with them. I try telling my heart that my children haven't been kidnapped but the screaming from the pain drowns out the controlled dispassionate voice of reason.

Here is a question:

What would you be willing to do to get your children back if someone stole them?

What would you *not* do to be with your children? What would be over the top? Too much to ask or consider? What would make a right minded parent say, "Nah, I will be better off without my children, keep em'?

Would you give an arm or a leg to be with your children?

Would you set your own hair on fire to get your daughter back?

Would you take out one of your own eyes if it meant that you could see your children again with the remaining one?

I was in the belly of the beast. I had not accepted the master plan. I was still waiting for justice, hoping for redemption and trying to make sense out of our situation while blindly flailing about: a fish on a hook in the bottom of the boat, struggling to no avail, a giant leap over the gunwales impossible.

Chapter 15: Where Are All the Dads Not?

I stopped at another restaurant for liquid. I wanted a tall one that I could swim in. It was about 8pm. There was a mother and grandmother and two children. The typical Costa Rican family: no father. I wondered where their father was and what his story was. How did he come to not be here on this Sunday night dinner?

I took a picture of myself as proof of the date. I had seen it done in a kidnapping movie. I held the day's newspaper up to my head and shot a photo of myself. It was the first time and last time I took out the camera on the entire trip.

I paid my check, turned on my flashlight and continued down the road.

Since I was little I loved flashlights. All little kids love flashlights. Sean, Ted and I had our own personal Maglites. We gave flashlights as presents when we went to little kid birthday parties.

Games

My favorite sound in the world is my children's laughter. I learned that playing Hide and Seek with flashlights, in the house, at night.

Although our house was small, any shadow is a hiding spot in total darkness. Even the obvious spots provided shelter from the seeker. Just a measure of invisibility is what we were seeking and finding.

The flashlight could pass directly over a person, it felt like the spotlights flashing in prison breaks with the excitement of the chase.

The game began as tradition dictated, "One, two, three...nine, ten! Ready or not heeere I coooome!"

Sean and Ted were both good hiders but their downfall was always the giggle. If I came too near, they would erupt with giggles. I ignored the giggle which would only cause more of the same. This night I ran my hands through the hanging clothes in the closet and found Sean first, sitting on the floor trying like mad to contain his laughter with hands clamped over a mouth in rebellion. Giggles start as nervousness and then turn compulsive, the mind wants to stop but the mouth keeps-on and the laughter has a life of its own.

I laughed in church when I was in seventh grade. I think someone farted or made a comment and I couldn't stop laughing until it became nervous and unstoppable, then obvious and distracting, until I was yanked by the collar by Sister Such and Such. I can relate to the compulsive giggle.

After I found Sean in the closet we went to look for Ted. We turned-off our flashlights and went in stealth. Ted was most likely in the basement. We crept down the stairs making sure to step on the outside of each riser to avoid the squeak of the 60 year old wood.

This game taught us patience. It taught us not to be afraid of the dark and it taught us to trust all our senses and not just our eyes. To do well in the game, the seeker had to be methodical and the hider had to develop the emotional self-control to stifle the giggle.

We challenged ourselves by only using a red flashlight. Red light allows night vision to remain functional, but illuminates less. It is like a video game visual of the world under the red spot light.

The thrill was seeing the red light of the seeker coming closer, holding your breathe and resisting the urge to laugh out loud. The hider could always see when the seeker was coming. The hider had this counterintuitive advantage. They were in the know but the seeker was lost: Lost with a light. Sometimes it is better in the dark. You can see more and take advantage. It was so dark that a person could move through a room without the seeker even noticing, like I am moving through the lives of my children, without them even noticing.

I talked while I was seeking and looking back on it, that was unfair. If we had the chance to play the game today, I think we should outlaw talking by the seeker. There should be no psychological warfare.

I feel like we have been playing hide and seek for the last four years and the psychological warfare has been devastating for all.

Someday we will be in contact again. I am seeking and I will not give up. I don't have a flashlight and I wish my children knew I was looking for them. They don't know what I have done and what I am willing to do to be a father, present in their everyday lives.

Sean, Ted, Elizabeth…Ready or not…here I come.

Chapter 16: Giving Up.

After walking for fifteen hours, I checked-in to the hotel around 10pm. Exhausted does not describe my state. My legs were knots. I hobbled to the room and let my clothes fall off. I showered till I felt guilty about wasting water and lay in bed in a towel.

I was in Alajuela and close to my goal but I just couldn't walk. I lathered the Bed-Gay product and slept deeply like the dead. I was going to make it. I would prove my will.
"Hail Mary, full of grace...."

Day Three.

Alajuela to San Jose Center

6am to 4pm

10 hours

Eyes wide open. Pain wide open.

"Hail Mary..." Four times.

On the morning of the third day the road had no compassion. I focused on each pebble because any jagged rock, no matter how small, sent a sharp pain through the already broken blisters. Raw feet and stiff muscles would be my downfall. I ate bananas and peanuts and passed the Dos Pinos (Two Pines) milk refinery. This stretch of road from Alajuela **to** San Jose would be long and straight and gravelly with high traffic volume at close range.

After about two hours, I hobbled to a gas station and lay in the grass, considering my options.

I gave up.

The highway from Alajuela to San Jose.

I was a wifeless husband and father to fatherless children in a foreign land. I was not permitted to leave the country or work legally, yet I was forced to somehow provide money under threat of incarceration. I was lying on the side of a highway at mid-morning, unable to move without pain.

I thought about the last two years of my life and all the decisions I made attempting to keep my family together and to avoid the place where I found myself on that day: alone and exiled from my family.

The previous two years looked like this…

Part II

You Can't Make People Happy

September 8, 2009 – July 29, 2011

Chapter 1: Lack of Sleep.

Elizabeth was born on 9/8/09. After two weeks, Soledad was exhausted. Lack of sleep is a form of torture. The mind goes loopy and decisions and reality all warp into fun house mirrors.

At the end of the Navy SEAL program, there is a "Hell Week" training event. During this time all the various physical challenges are endured except through the final test, the candidates are deprived of sleep. Even the most determined individuals in the world break from lack of sleep, the remaining few become SEALs.

How could we expect my wife not to be affected by physical exhaustion?

Soledad was particularly enormous of belly when carrying Elizabeth. After two births of big boys: Sean 8lbs, 10 ounces; Ted 9lbs, my wife's stomach muscles were able to stretch-out to proportions bordering ridiculous and because of this unnatural girth, she could not sleep well in any one position for more than an hour or two until she either had to use the bathroom or simply wake up to roll herself over.

She was also plagued with acid reflux. She had to be very careful what she ate or she would be paying with a mouth full of acid and a burning stomach.

Apart from her girth and lack of sleep Soledad was still managing the house and two young boys. By the time that Elizabeth was born, Soledad had not had a full night's sleep for four months.

Breastfeeding is a beautiful process: natural, bonding, life giving. Yadda yadda yadaa…Breastfeeding in practice can be torture. My wife was tortured with the pain of bleeding nipples and a hungry mouth. She would cry with anticipation of the pain, and those first seconds when she knew the pain was eminent, the grimace, the clenched eyes, the sounds of sucking in through her teeth and then the exhale as Elizabeth began.

I saw my wife was slowing down, becoming more silent, and spending as much time as possible in bed.

I asked if she thought she was, "getting depressed."

She weakly said, "Yes." As if ashamed it was happening again, against her will. Post-Partum had crept in.

At week three my wife's tone of voice changed. She said she wanted a divorce and she wanted me to leave the house. It was simple for her. I was the problem and if I went away, the problem would go away.

It was then I started backpedaling and here is what I did by using the only tool in my box, the practical slide rule, for the next year and two months. That single-minded practical approach contributed to the transformation from what I thought was love and commitment into utter disdain, infidelity and ultimately the kidnapping of our children.

Chapter 2: Time on the Floor.

Soledad was stressed because she was waking me up in the middle of the night feeding Elizabeth. I didn't have a problem but the fact that I didn't feel stress was not the point, she was feeling stress.

What could I do to relieve any of that stress?

I remember when Sean was a newborn I took one of the feeding shifts in the middle of the night.

I took the 3am shift, crept into the bedroom, pulled him to my chest and he stopped crying. I heated wet wipes in the microwave for exactly three seconds so they would be warm on his bottom. Those were magical nights of bonding for father and son. I sang the same song softly three times, until he went back to sleep. "Rock-a-bye Sean, on the tree top, when the wind blows…"

Looking back, I don't know why I would want Sean to think that his cradle was on a tree-top, but he loved the tone and I loved singing to my son in the cool dark quiet hours until he slept, then slipping from the room on cold tip toes to return to sleep before school.

Singing to Ted

When Teddyboy was born there was a problem with his urethra. The result was that when he peed, the liquid would get stuck. He needed an operation.

This experience in the Costa Rica hospital was before we lived the trials of Childhood Cancer with Sean. Our baby boy Teddy needed an operation. He was only a few months old, which is dangerous enough. Secondly, they were operating on this penis. All kinds of bad things can go wrong apart from death, like a life with a bad willy and all the trauma that can cause.

Soledad and I stood in the small room at the Children's Hospital of Costa Rica. The sheets were a blood stained grey from the previous users. The room felt dirty, like it could never be clean, the paint, drab as prison issue underpants, clung to the walls for fear of falling to the scarred tiled floor. What looked like molding, where wall meets floor, was just the dark shadow of past mop marks.

Teddy's song was a simple repetition of his name: Teddyboy, Teddyboy… Teddyboy, Teddyboy.

It went on in a meditative tone for days.

It wasn't the words; it was the emotion, the rhythm and the tone.

Umm Kalthum is an Egyptian Singer who died in 1975. She is known as the greatest Arabic singer. Her range and strength were superior. She would sing songs for 45 minutes, 90 minutes, 3 hours, always repeating a sing phrase while toying with the emotions and nuance of emphasis.

I sang the Teddyboy Song to him (and for me) in the hospital.

The little girl in the bed next to Ted asked her mother to sing her the song. The girl's father wasn't around. I felt sorry for her. Where were the fathers in this country? He must be a coward or drunk, I thought.

Lord, forgive me for my judgment.

Chapter 3: October 29, 2009.

I didn't offer to take a nighttime feeding shift with Elizabeth; maybe I should have. This story, like any, is ripe with "could have's" and "should have's" and we are left with the decisions we made at the time and we live with the results.

I offered to sleep on the floor in the boys' room so Soledad and Elizabeth could sleep and feed as they wished. It was a big mistake leaving the marital bed. I knew that, but my hubris convinced me that our relationship was strong enough. We weren't. The wheels fell off. I never made it back to the marital bed.

This was the first big step towards the end of our marriage. I now recognize the emotion that kicked the snowball down the hill was hubris. I thought I could help my wife, and guide our lives towards a path of familial happiness.

I suffer hubris no more, but like each component that contributed to the destruction of the life that I created and lost, hubris took its own pound of flesh.

"Pride goeth before the fall," and my plummet has been three years in the descent. I have touched bottom and am rocketing towards the surface once again, reborn, phoenix like, in search of a relationship with my children as I reflect on components that lead to our separation.

While sleeping on the floor, I got to share more time with my sons. We read, went to sleep and woke together and our relationship grew with our bunking time.

Four months I slept on the floor between my son's beds. I didn't mind at all.

* 9/29/09: Soledad contacts Dan Knight, a former love interest, through Facebook. She tells him of her abusive husband. He is coming off the heels of a divorce. They chat for hours. She tells

him she "has been waiting for him for 20 years." Elizabeth is 7 weeks old.

Note: An asterisk (*) will here on out, indicate information not known to John P. Murphy at the time, but later provided by Dan Knight in 2014 through interviews, personal emails, airline receipts, wire transfer receipts and photographs.

Chapter 4: Taking Over.

I thought my wife needed more rest and less stress. The work to maintain a house is a full time gig. Just the laundry for five people is a part-time job.

I always had a share in the laundry duties but then I took over the duties and maybe that is my message here. I "took over." I separated, washed, dried, folded and put away. She had zero responsibility for the never ending task. "She's gotta' appreciate me lightening the load," thought the practical man I was.

I was already in charge of grocery shopping. On Saturdays, Sean and Ted and I woke early and silently slipped out to Produce Palace to leave my wife and Elizabeth to sleep. Produce Palace is run by Spanish speaking folk, so we practiced our Spanish while there. We looked at flowers and bought fruits for Teddyboy.

We then went to the super market together and bought the 8 bags worth of goods that a family of five mows through in a week. We made it home by noon and unpacked our wares including treats for Mamá. We never came back without bringing Swiss Chocolate, Milano Orange Cookies or flowers for Soledad.

I thought that taking on all the shopping duties would help.

Soledad didn't need her practical load lighter; she needed an Emotional Tai Chi Master: A person who could recognize her feelings and emotions and not react to the tidal wave, but let that negative energy drift past. She needed me to let the emotions pass, but I was a practical boxer and had not yet even earned a white belt as an Emotional Tai Chi Student.

I approached conflict with useless logic. When her ire was up, instead of taking a step back and accepting the barrage, I often took offense or pointed out weakness in her argument. My Brute Irish nature rose to any occasion and met conflict with conflict, surging energy with more energy to arrive at a point of negative communication: the ultimate disaster in a relationship.

If I had then what I know now, if I were the man then that I am now, my children might have a had a better shot at a two parent household, but we all have our lives to live and the universe doesn't make mistakes. We generate what we need and I needed to feel profound emotional pain for an extended period of time to arrive at a positive now.

My children, for reasons only known to God and the Universe, needed to be separated from their father to develop some part of their cosmic karma. This separation was necessary for all of our spiritual paths and like it or not: Life Is.

It took me over two years to realize that the more I did around the house, the worse my wife felt. For my wife, my hard work only highlighted her own insecurities. Among other things, she hates me for her feeling that way. I didn't know it at the time. I just kept taking on more household/childcare responsibilities and left her to bed and computer. I thought if I happily took more work away she would have time to rest and recuperate.

I was emotionally shortsighted.

So, I cleaned the bathrooms and vacuumed, cooked and was the full time dish washer. About every night, Sean, Ted and I swept the floors and made sure the house was tip top for Soledad in the morning. The recuperation of our marriage would just take some time and patience and tireless hard work.

Hard work? That is what we Irish Catholics do, it is what my father and mother did. There is another Irish Catholic path: drink and drink until all the money is gone, like the father of Frankie McCourt, (read <u>Angela's Ashes</u> for the drunken Irish story). Turns out, the hard work path that I chose would lead to the same end as the Drunk Irish path: fatherless children.

It is ironic that the wives of drunk husbands stick with em' while the sober, hardworking guys find their wives schtoopin' the mailman. Life works in a similar fashion for wives who do everything for their husbands and still find themselves on the receiving end of a backhand or runner-up to the secretary.

We were certainly in the "for worse," part of our martial vows. I reminded my wife of our vows one night when she asked me to leave the house. I said that we swore we would, "be together for better or for worse until death do us part," and that this is one of those rough times, but this too shall pass.

From the moment I walked in the door from school, the boys were with me until they went to sleep at night and all weekend long from the moment they woke on Saturday until we went to sleep on Sunday night, we were together.

Months passed like this: Soledad building a great wall of resentment and me trying to keep the show on the road by managing practical matters but not boring deeper into my wife's emotional state.

I said to Soledad that I would do anything to keep us together. "Leave the house," was the only response she gave me until February. I was three months into living with her disdain and was hopeful that with love and patience we could recover the equilibrium in our marriage. We had three children together and Sean survived childhood cancer. Giving up wasn't in my playbook. I would continue to drop back and punt. I'm Irish Catholic. Like I said, apart from hitting the bottle hard, I didn't know any other way existed. Initiating a divorce was not in my playbook.

In February, Soledad asked me for three things: Quit smoking cigarettes, quit smoking marijuana and read more to the boys.

I smoked one or two cigarettes a day and months had passed since I had smoked marijuana. I was an infrequent smoker at best. "That's it," I thought confidently.

"Done," I said. That was nowhere near a deal breaker. That was a piece of cake. I am good with clear limits. I quit that day. I mean not one cigarette and staying away from marijuana was a non-issue. It wasn't in my life. I read to the boys and Elizabeth every night.

That was easy, now everything will start to come back together and stop falling more apart.

Soledad still loathed my presence. She stopped participating in Family Meetings and did her best to be civil to me.

It was so hard for her. She was filled with this hate and she believed I was the cause. Hers was a difficult position. My position was no less challenging. I didn't smoke or drink on any regular basis. I didn't watch football or play golf. I worked, came right home, fathered and house made, what I didn't do well enough was love my wife.

The last words I spoke for 7 years before I went to sleep, every night: "I love you very much."

I kissed my wife when I arrived and left the house. I did the shabby best I could.

I don't know who could have made it through but I believe someone could have loved her better. It wasn't going to be me and I could accept that. The most challenging part would not be that Soledad didn't love me. Frankly, I didn't care about that. Great big blinking letters scan across the pages of my mind: You didn't care that your wife didn't love you? I cared little of the marriage. I didn't think I could ever satisfy my wife.

I wanted to be the father present in the everyday lives of my children. By the Law of Reverse Results, life gave me what I feared most and desired least: I would be present for nothing in the lives of Sean, Ted and Elizabeth; I was to become a memory, fading and muted.

* November 2009: Soledad and Dan Knight have declared their love for one another. They enter into a monogamous relationship with him swearing off women and her swearing off me. Soledad tells him she is leaving her abusive husband.

All that time I was doing housework, she was on the computer chatting with her lover. She begins planning how to manipulate the system to "get rid" of me, keep Dan and the kids and a house with alimony.

It was easy to do if you know a sliver of Costa Rican Culture and have no problem with lying.

Step One: Initiate a paper trail of domestic violence. The best source is a police report but since I never gave my wife a reason to call the police, she went to the next best source, a woman's shelter, where she could get a letter stating she received domestic violence counseling.

Chapter 5: Soledad's Class.

In March, Soledad enrolled in a course to gain her teaching certificate in New Jersey. She reasoned if she could get a job teaching, she would then have the money to leave me. I supported her decision. I followed Stephen Covey and 10,000 Maniacs. "Hey, give em´ what they want. If lust and hate is the candy. If blood and love taste so sweet...then we...Give em' want they want" (10,000 Maniacs, 1992).

Soledad wanted her certificate. I embraced the decision even though the end result would be for her to leave me. The alternative is to deny her the funding and assistance necessary to achieve her goal. There would be no positive result there. I would be an oppressor, which I am not, so I didn't.

The course was at a New Jersey Community College near Trenton. It was about a 45 minute ride on highways with a bridge crossing and tolls. Soledad couldn't/wouldn't/felt she couldn't drive herself there. I realize that it is one thing to support a person and quite another to enable them. Now, I see myself as an enabler. I should have said, "If you want your certificate, then drive yourself there because when you get a teaching job you're going to be doing the driving."

That answer seems so obvious to me now only because of what I have learned from experience. At the time my belief that, "I will do anything for my wife," was put to the test and we Brute Irish Catholics love a test of wills. We simply excel at pointless acts of will.

I chauffeured my wife to her classes. My mother-in-law stayed at our house a few times to watch Elizabeth. I arrived home from school with just enough time to pee and make a roadie sandwich for the car. I mounted the mini-van with Ted, Sean and Soledad, and like a Sahara Rally Stop, I was back on the track with only a five minute turnaround for the next leg of my race: a rush hour 40 minute highway drive to the Trenton area.

While Soledad was in her class, Ted, Sean and I waited in a strip mall. We found salvation in a lost music store. We sat at a shiny gold drum kit and tapped light rhythm with whisk brushes. We tickled electric key boards until they laughed out loud their deep belly bass moans and little girl high notes, like crystal shattering on ice. We tapped copper cowbells and mooed; caressed the lithe necks of violins and pulled single sad high notes. The brassy trumpets lay sleeping in red velvet cases like kings in a bed.

Guitars, like women, have a unique form and size from the narrow necked bases to the full figured Mexicans.

We ate pizza at the supermarket and read Dr. Seuss and a picture Encyclopedia of Transportation. We read in the car, waiting for our queen to finish her class.

Twice, I took Elizabeth with us and this was all the more an adventure. We kept up our music routine and fed and changed Elizabeth along the way. I am doing everything the practical man should do to help his wife. I am happy with my life.

I proofread my wife's papers and sent her transcripts to be translated but I still had my doubts that she was eligible for New Jersey Emergency Certification in Spanish with a Tourism Degree from Costa Rica.

After six weeks of class and the waiting at the strip mall, at times in the rain and always at night, Soledad was not eligible for that certificate. We had wasted our time. My wife felt another door was closed on her and I, in-turn, felt her close another door on me.

"Jesus Christ, Lord have mercy on my soul."

Chapter 6: Marriage Counseling.

Spring 2010 was pushing its way into our lives and soon we would be swimming and biking. Soledad and I went to a marriage counselor.

His name was Mark and his home office was in New Hope. It is the quaintest of Bucks County Villages with theatre and gays and bikers and financially fruitful folk. He helped rich people solve imaginary problems and he drove a Porsche. He was in his late forties and enjoyed the comfort of being a sounding board. He had nothing to lose and risked very little. He sat in his slick grey leather art deco chair with matching ottoman, tapped his stocking feet together, clasped his hands on his paunch and with the expectant smile of the voyeur asked, "So what is going on?"

I had thought deeply on this question. What were we doing here? I had narrowed it down to a sentence. My true belief about why we are here:

I am seeking redemption.

Redemption is a return to a previous state of grace.

I then gave Mark some brass tacks to work with, to help us either tear apart or patch together our relationship. One of those brass tacks in my shoe was that I looked at pornography while masturbating. My wife didn't abide porn or wanking. She considered that infidelity. We went through the basics of who we are and from whence we came.

His one poignant question was whether my wife wanted to, "save our marriage." She said, "I don't know. I don't think so."

Our ship started sinking that day, because if your lover feels the relationship is over, effort will never change the timbre of their heartstrings. You can't make someone love you and you can't make someone happy. You can't even satisfy someone who doesn't want it. No matter what you do.

The more you try, the worse they may hate you. My misguided acts of will caused the opposite of the intended result; I was only further alienating my wife. She kept on hating me more, that's for sure. My trying hard in practical household matters was totally misdirected. My wife cared nothing of practical matters, she cared about how she felt and we were ill equipped to handle those emotions. Each job I took-on hoping to help my wife only added ballast to the already sinking ship.

To Mark the counselor, I mentioned that my wife suffered from Postpartum Depression (PPD) after our first two children and that she was affected by lack of sunlight in the winter time (SADD) and had not had a full night's sleep in about 8 months. Mentioning Postpartum Depression sets off outrage and indignation. For a woman with PPD, even presenting the idea as a possibility is tinder for an argument. It is one of God's little jokes.

Soledad was still painfully struggling with breastfeeding Elizabeth. At seven months old, Elizabeth had not yet slept through the night. Soledad continued to rise at all hours to feed Elizabeth and she was a zombie most of the time. We spoke at length on more than one occasion about following a similar method as we had with Ted and Sean.

We let our boys cry, believing that the ability to self-sooth is a learned skill. Also, we didn't sleep in the same bed with Sean and Ted. We napped together but when Soledad finished breast feeding the boys, we returned them to their crib, so everybody slept in their own bed, not so with Elizabeth.

Elizabeth and Soledad slept together fitfully each night and nothing was going to change my wife's mind about her decisions. She wasn't going to be convinced by me, expert advice or our own experience with breastfeeding and sleeping. She was tired and her decision making process was not cutting edge but she possessed self-assurance in plentitude. It is a dangerous combination turned fatal for a couple with an insecure husband who seeks approval.

Counselor Mark avoided addressing the postpartum issue. I understand that he was hesitant to take risks and lose trust. He just let us get it all out.

We didn't talk about our emotions and fears and he didn't ask. I can't imagine going to a counselor and not addressing fears and emotions but I was so much older then, I'm younger than that now.

*Soledad never mentioned in our counseling sessions that she had declared her undying love to another man and that they promised they would, "never leave each other," and that all she had to do was, "get rid of somebody." The quotes are from chat conversations between Dan Knight and Soledad, given to me by Dan Knight four years after the fact.

Soledad manipulates the counselor. Had she told the truth of her affair at any time, our story could be very different.

Chapter 7: Center of my World.

I lose things. Since I was little I lost things. Chalk it up to irresponsibility, ADD, or poor parenting, but at the end of the day, responsibility statements always begin with the word, "I."
I lose things.

I have installed systems in my life and have been since called "organized" by colleagues and students. I was not born organized, I learned how to help myself and use techniques that minimize my problems with misplacing items.

The "Center of My World," is a bowl that I place on a table next to the front door of wherever I have lived or slept for the past 20 years. When I travel to friend's houses for visits and they ask me if I "need anything," I reply that I could use a bowl. I place my driver's license, cell phone, credit cards, keys, change and folding money in that bowl and I feel like I am at home -my universe "centered."

My cell phone is with me, in the bowl or charging in the ONE place that I use to charge my phone. I leave that cord in its designated spot. I have seen organized folk do the same.

I was taken by surprise, when my cell did not materialize, in the "merry, merry month of May."

I asked Soledad if she had seen my phone and she told me with some disdain that, "You probably lost it again."

Touché. Maybe I deserve that reproach since I couldn't find the phone. I was sure it was charging. I said, "Boy, I really felt like I left it charging," with as much Holden Caulfield gosh-darn humility as I could muster.

Although I hadn't been in the van yet that week, I took one last search through the van because remotes and phones are always lurking under the seats, whether it is in the car or in the den.

I found the phone hidden in a compartment in the center console. I didn't even know this compartment existed. My wife had stolen my phone and hidden it. I was deflated; I didn't think that people really did that type of thing outside of Mexican soap operas.

I went back inside with the phone and showed it to my wife. I asked if any strange calls or texts had arrived from mysterious women. No phone calls from women? Nothing?

There were no other women. Suspicion of others is the work of a guilty conscience. The thief thinks everyone steals and the cheater suspects everyone of cheating.

The topic of my integrity came up during one of the marriage counseling sessions. I felt that the sessions had become a "John Bashing" parade. I sat and listened and contributed defenses and thoughts.

In the sessions, we never talked about the integrity of a person who invades another's privacy, nor more importantly, did we strike upon the emotions (fears) that caused my wife to steal my phone and lie to me. That would have been real progress and worthy of $150 an hour. No, we stayed right on the surface of our problems and our psychologist continued to tap his stocking feet, offering nothing.

I was wishing we had talked more about the right to privacy when two years later I learned a new word: Keylogger.

Chapter 8: What I Thought was Consensus.

We were sitting in the kitchen on a Saturday Spring morning in 2010; Soledad hating me and me trying to avoid conflict and hoping that with enough patience Soledad would come out of the tailspin and recognize that life just wasn't so bad.

We had considered remodeling the kitchen a few months before but had decided against it. Soledad accused me of being "controlling." She had wanted to re-model the kitchen but she said, "your mother talked you out of it."

I sat down and said, "Wow, I didn't know I was being controlling. I thought we arrived at a consensus that it wasn't the right time to redo the kitchen." It was sunny in the morning, there was a light breeze and the gossamer white curtains breathed new life in and out.

I thought that we had identified a "short" in our communication. If Soledad viewed our decisions as me dictating then I could take a new approach and address this basic miscommunication. My wife would then feel more empowered because we are clearly defining agreement, disagreement and consensus.

What initially smelled like fresh progress later stunk of repeated failure.

I suggested we bring that decision to remodel the kitchen back up for discussion. I was open to remodeling the kitchen.

I told Soledad that I could go to the bank right now and get the money. "Let's do it!" I said with enthusiasm that didn't spread.

No, it was too late. She didn't want a new kitchen.

It felt like any effort I made to correct a situation was too little, too late and never met with an open mind.

A new or old kitchen wasn't the problem, it was her emotional state tied into what the kitchen represented. We needed to remodel the kitchen of our emotions.

But I didn't know how, I didn't even know what I didn't know. I wore practical blinders.

In direct proportion to my willingness change course, Soledad expressed her will by remaining steadfast in her disdain. I would get to know her will and disdain intimately over the next three years and the extremes of which she is capable.

I could never have fathomed her capacity for lies and manipulation, nor the self-destruction that followed.

Chapter 9: Time Apart, Time to Cry.

By the spring of 2010, my wife had hated me for eight months strong.

There was not a day of mercy or a moment of weakness. I don't say that as a victim, I say it with empathy. It is hard on the body and spirit and mind to despise the presence of a person with whom you share a home and children.

Eight months I had been backpedaling and hoping for a turnaround. I was committed to family and frankly, the love I received and the happiness of being a father far outweighed the emotions of my wife. If she hated me, that was her problem, I could live with her hate. It wasn't great, but it wasn't so bad either. I loved being a father. I would eat a mile of shite to experience the pleasure of fatherhood.

And that was my problem; I could live with her hate. I wasn't going to leave. I still hoped that we could reconcile and I was willing to wait because I remembered the year before Elizabeth was born when we didn't have one harsh word between us. Everything was ostensibly perfect with our lives. I thought this disaster started with Postpartum Depression and I wasn't going to forget the time before the storm when I felt we were in an eternal spring. What I didn't understand so well was that my wife couldn't live with her hate.

Soledad was eaten up. She had done all she could to get me to leave. Made life hard with hate and she made hoops and I eagerly jumped through them. She wanted her teaching cert and I had helped with that process, she wanted counseling and I was an advocate for a mediator. Now, she wanted time apart. She wanted to go to Costa Rica for a month and she wanted to leave now. She upped the ante by setting the hoops on fire, so I put on my Teflon underpants and made ready to jump. Drumroll please.

I suppose that many people would not have allowed her to leave the country with the children for fear that she would not return. I didn't have that fear. I continued to act in a manner that gave her what she needed. I am no saint nor am I remarkably stupid.

I believe deeply in the philosophy of non-controlling love: Love that is strong enough to allow the other person to find their own happiness. Maybe she would find her happiness and I would not be included in the picture. I could accept that as well.

How could I live for a month without Sean, Ted and Elizabeth? My identity was father, husband, and teacher. My role as a husband always took a back seat to fatherhood. We put our marriage behind the needs of the children and with the effort we did make with our marriage, we only accomplished practical band aids....go on a date night, watch a movie together, give kisses and hugs in plentitude and say, "I love you all the time." We just never addressed how we were feeling or why we were feeling that way.

We bought the tickets for Soledad, Sean, Ted and Elizabeth to visit Costa Rica.

With the limited knowledge I had, I thought that maybe time apart would help.

It was then that I started having uncontrollable tears. I cried every day throughout the day that my family was gone. I was not used to being alone. I was not used to the lack of physical contact.

I didn't have a life outside my children. We did everything together. They were my shadows. We bathed and showered and slept and ate together. If I was not working Sean and Ted were with me.

When I visited friends and family during this time most made the same comment: "I don't think I've ever seen you without the boys since you've been back from Costa Rica."

I decided to remodel the kitchen and put a bathroom in the basement. Home Depot became my second home where I learned the loneliness of the old man. My whole life I had seen old people, men mostly, wandering through stores buying nothing and making small talk with whomever would listen. They were lonely, there was an empty house waiting and they had not had a conversation with anyone the whole blessed day.

I found myself attempting humor at the Acme Supermarket with the guy collecting the carts at the end of the night or the Garden Department crew rolling in the Bar-B-Que grills at Lowe's. I would talk to anyone and if they engaged me, there would inevitably be a point at the end of fluid conversation where they would say, "Alright then, I'm gonna get back to work."

I walked to my car and cried tears of the lonely fool. I glimpsed a possible future, 80 years old with sagging pants held up only by the power of suspenders, a hanky in my back pocket and an aged John Deer hat, wandering the wide aisles and concrete floors of super hardware stores looking for a friend with whom to talk.

On the 16th of July, I spoke with Soledad. The papers that she forgot to take with her, which I had sent to her brother's Florida post office box, had not arrived in Costa Rica. Soledad was getting Elizabeth's Residence Card for Costa Rica and was highly agitated that the papers had not arrived and more specifically, that it was my fault.

I had long since accepted I could be brought to blame for any situation. I was an easy target.

I could accept this premise for one reason: I thought my wife was not well. The person who hated me and hated her life was not the woman I married. My goal was to do everything within my power to help my wife regain some emotional stability, but I employed practical means to do so. I didn't even know what I didn't know about emotions. I thought with enough love, listening, patience, and hard work, we could eventually arrive on common ground with a single vision of our future as a family.

So, when my wife said she wanted to stay in Costa Rica another two weeks, I said, "OK." I cried hot tears and gulped air in big man draughts. Another two weeks without my children.

"Give the one you love what they need." I lived by that principle and coped with the ensuing emotional pain by praying.

Prayer was the only escape from the reality that surrounded me. I could only quiet my mind by using the Jesus Prayer: Dear Lord, Jesus Christ, have mercy on my soul.

I said Hail Mary's all day. I would pray constantly, anywhere, in English and in Spanish.

I had hope; hope and Hail Mary's.

My family arrived home after 6 weeks. My children and I hugged tight and long. My wife stood, unsmiling and distant.

Six weeks of work and $15,000 and her response was perfect, now, knowing that life is a comedy, I should have expected it. I wasn't disappointed with her answer; it just marked another thing that didn't work.

"The porch is dusty. This looks like a kitchen for a bachelor."

She still hated me. Darn.

It had been about ten months and nothing I had tried had affected a positive change of heart or attitude from my wife.

This ship is going down. I stood at the helm; vest less, as the water rose above my ankles.

"Hail Mary, full of grace, the Lord is with you..."

* Soledad used this time apart to consummate her extramarital affair. Dan Knight also travelled to Costa Rica. Dan and Soledad and the children went on a vacation to the beach. Dan slept in the same bed as Soledad and Elizabeth. Ted and Sean slept in the next room. I had been replaced.

When the family returned to the U.S., I asked Ted about their trip. He said, "We met Mamá's friend." I said, "Uncle Pablo" and he said, "No." I then said, "Uncle Diego" and he said, "No." With my interest peeked, Soledad came rushing into the room and squashed the conversation. She dismissed a confused Ted, then told me that I was being controlling, having to know every detail of their trip.

She had now involved the children in her hidden betrayal. We would all play pawns to her fears born of hidden betrayal and outright lies.

Sean, Ted and Elizabeth are still living as pawns, under the false pretenses of a distorted reality.

Chapter 10: A Need for Approval.

You can't change someone's perspective, only they can. You can mount defenses but if someone believes, someone believes, and that is the end of that story.

As a teacher, I valued the time that I was able to spend with my children during the summer. We had achieved bicycle freedom and since the boys return, we doubled our fun with water safety and swimming. We held our breath and lived briefly like dolphins underwater. We spent our time outside, on adventures, shopping or visiting friends and parks.

Soledad spent most of her time in front of a computer or in bed watching television or napping with Elizabeth. Elizabeth girl was beginning to wean, but was still not sleeping through those nights. My wife and Elizabeth lived separate lives from the boys and me.

The boys learned to swim that summer. We had three swimming starts: Mike's pool, the Olinger's pool and the bathtub. Mike's pool sat unguarded on the right side of his house next to the two bay garage. It was one of those popular three foot deep inflatable pools with a 15' diameter.

The summer before Soledad moved the children to Costa Rica permanently, Sean and Ted and I would go to Mike's house almost every day and when the fall set in, we would go to Mike's pool in the afternoon when I got home from school.

The game at Mike's pool started about 10 yards from the pool where the fire pit had burnt its dried earth stamp on the lawn like a buffalo wallowing hole. Sean and Ted got a running start and charged at the pool and since the sides of the blue pool were flexible plastic with a soft bumper edge, they jumped, bumped their chest on the soft edge and slid into the pool. And again, running start and dive and running start and dive and running start and dive until a worn wet path was carved on trampled grass.

Each run was a new thrill. I can still hear the boys saying, "Papá watch me," before each run.

I have that same need for approval. It was like something didn't happen to me if somebody wasn't aware of my effort. I also worked from the perilous premise of, "making my wife happy."

I was always so proud of my accomplishment but at the same time, as I reflect now, I had a need for approval. I thrive on it and as young boys who looked up to their father, they too had that same desire. Maybe all little kids have that desire. I just never grew out of it.

Approval seeking behavior is weak and smells of insecurity. If a person is secure, they have no need to seek the approval of anyone but themselves. I have since grappled with needing approval. I now do things for myself, smile and let them pass. The pleasure of someone giving me an unsolicited compliment is far greater than pointing out how great I am myself. Life is a process.

We played Marco Polo in the small pool. Calling out, "Marco" and diving in the direction of the "Polo" response as that person ducked under to swim away. Escape left a wake in the water. We sensed the other person from the draft created by bodies moving through water. I believe this memoir will create a draft of energy that someday my children will follow and that one day we will find each other anew.

"Marco!"

"Polo."

This was the last summer that we were together. Soledad had been asking me to leave the house for 10 months since Elizabeth was born. She never used the word divorce; she just wanted me to leave. I refused, neither from spite, nor the financial risk of "abandoning" the home but because of all the moments that we (Sean, Ted and Elizabeth and I) spent together. These moments were invaluable to me and I would do anything to be with my children and help them in this life. I could withstand the disdain of my wife but she could not stand her disdain for me. To me, those moments learning to swim had a greater value than suffering the hate of my wife. For my wife, there was nothing worth enduring my presence.

That last summer Sean and Ted learned to ride bicycles. In those waning days of summer, Soledad still wanted me to leave the house. I realized that if I had left three months before, my children would not know how to swim or how to ride a bicycle. I was determined to hang-in to the very end so I could give my children all the gifts and skills that I possibly could.

My wife did not have a father who was present in her life. Her mother separated from her father at the same time Soledad was leaving me, when she and Tia Carla were 3 and 4.

Soledad can neither swim nor ride a bike.

"Marco?"

"Marco?"

"Marco!?"

We are still playing the same game.

*My wife spent hours on the computer every day, chatting with her next husband. She was now acting as his personal assistant to completely entrench herself in his life and the life they were creating together. She arranged for his flight to Spain to have a stop-over in Philadelphia, where they fornicated in the white family minivan in the airport parking lot.

I was trying to figure out how to help our marriage and she was bangin' her bo' in the back a' the van.

Chapter 11: My Wife in Counseling.

Summer to fall in 2010, a new school year, Ted is 4, Elizabeth turns 1, Sean turns 6, it is my third year teaching at Urban Academy Charter High School and my wife has despised me for more than one year.

My wife quit counseling with Psychologist Mark but I had not given up. I wanted to hear a female perspective, so I found just that: a mature female psychologist with grey in her hair and smile wrinkles around her eyes and mouth. She sat and listened and I told her my tale. She wore Birkenstocks and Eddie Bauer; she was widowed and had known loss. She was privileged Jewish, cultured and I was hoping she could give me insight on methods I could employ to build bridges with my wife.

Once again, I got a lot of head shaking and agreement. It was all but a waste of time.

My wife then accused me of having Anger Management problems and that is one of her justifications for her actions over the past three years. I have taken the tests to see where I fall on the scale of Anger Management. Each test I took I never even came close. Even when I went with the perspective of her answering the questions for me I never arrived in the scale of Anger Management.

Anger Management was just another hoop I would jump through only to have the hoop moved. I was Charlie Brown and I just kept trying to kick that ball. It is laughable how naïve I was (am?).

However, there was a method to my naiveté, I tested my principles. Would I be willing to do anything so as to allow my wife to find her personal happiness? Yes, I was, I allowed my wife her desires to the point of allowing her to leave the country, a giant leap of faith but after three years of free fall I have landed catlike on my feet. I tested my beliefs' system in the flesh and blood of action and triumphed as a result. It was a long and sometimes lonely road to get here but I have arrived at a place where I am secure in my convictions and seek the approval of no man or court system. I am a better man for it.

Going to the counseling sessions alone was futile. Without a willing partner to work on the problems together, we were going to get nowhere but further apart.

One night in early October there was a voicemail message from a Psychologist for Soledad. She hadn't told me that she was seeing any counselors. When I asked her about the message she was indignant and told me that it was, "none of my business" and that I was, "being controlling by asking her about it."

We were in the bedroom, she was in bed, it was twilight and I was in my school clothes. I continued to play the guy in the white hat. I never wanted to take that hat off. I told her that she didn't have to talk to me about her counseling session. It didn't matter to me what she was doing or where she was going. I was happy that she was getting help.

What difference could it make to me? She was getting help. I was thrilled. She was making an effort to get us out of the garbage heap where our marriage had been for a year.

I tentatively put my hand on her knee and said, "I am so glad you are getting help. If there is anything I can do or if at some point I could go with you, I am willing to do whatever."

I had a thought that we would be OK. I had faith that with patience and perseverance and listening and communicating that we would soon move into the, "for better" part of our marriage.

Again, darn, I could not have been more wrong.

Seven months later when I arrived in Costa Rica to rejoin my family, the police delivered a Restraining Order against me. I found out the name of the place where my wife was going for counseling in the U.S.

A simple letter with the name of the organization was enough to remove me from my children's lives for a whole year:

"A Woman's Place: Domestic Violence Counseling."

Chapter 12: Gone at 500 Miles per Hour.

When the leaves fell in 2010, Sean, Ted and I gathered them into massive piles and dove into the golden mounds, all crisp like thin paper. We slept outside in a large tent. We roasted marshmallows in the fire pit and drifted to sleep with the sounds of the waterfall from the pond.

In late October, Soledad and I sat in the kitchen when she told me that she had to leave the U.S. She was not well, hadn't been mentally well for over a year now, I thought. My wife was slowly dying and each of my efforts to help our situation failed.

She wanted to go to visit her sister Carla in Spain and then return to live in Costa Rica. She wanted to leave in three weeks and be in Spain for Christmas. I asked her if we could spend Christmas together in the U.S.

She said, "I will not be sane by Christmas."

Foolishly, I asked if she could make it to the end of my school year in June. We would all finish our schooling together and could leave as a family.

She said, "I will not be alive by June if I have to stay here."

The core of my beliefs was about to be put to the test. Would I be willing to live without my children for 6 months for the benefit of my wife's mental health?

Soledad classified her leaving as, "a step towards reconciliation." I could, "visit Spain for Christmas together and then visit Costa Rica during the Easter Holidays," she said.

I cried silently and told her that if that is what she needed then I could do this for her. I cried every day when the children were gone for 6 weeks; the idea of six months shook me. It scared me to my core but I was willing "to pass through the shadow of the valley of death because I feared no evil." Actually, I feared the hell out of evil but I kept walking just the same.

We bought plane tickets and I started to prep the boys for our separation.

There were so many factors to consider and I went to all my sources for advice.

I asked my wife what the worst case scenario was for us. I was concerned that she would get used to not having me around and when I arrived in Costa Rica she would want a divorce.

She said that the worst case scenario was that we would divorce and that I would see the children every other weekend and three times during the week.

I cried hard. I was sitting in the living room and I tried to imagine not putting Sean and Ted and Elizabeth to bed. I imagined not waking up every day with my children, not being there when they got home from school and all the "nots"…I would "not be there" for *everything* most of the time. I would only be there every other weekend and three times during the week.

I sat and cried. My wife left the room.

"Hail Mary, full of grace, the Lord is with thee…"

I talked to my parents and my brothers and sister; I asked friends whose opinion I trusted. Almost everyone told me I was a fool.

I decided to live and die by my principles.

My family left in a whirlwind for Spain. The house was a disaster from packing.

I kissed everyone at the airport.

My wife hugged me. It was the first time I heard her voice without an undertone of resentment and disdain in over a year. She sounded normal again. I had hope. I had heard her voice! She said, "Thank you John."

"Blessed art thou among women…"

It was 23 November 2010. Four years have passed since that afternoon when my children and my life all flew away. My identity rattled and banged: it was being drug behind the plane like tin cans roped to a "Just Married" car.

My children flew out of my life at 500 miles an hour.

There goes that life forever. I just didn't know it at the time.

I had hope. She said, "Thank you."

Everything is going to be fine. She'll come around.

"Hail Mary, full of grace…"

*My family briefly stayed with her sister, then Soledad and the children moved into Dan Knight's small apartment. She told him she had left me for good. She just hadn't told me yet and I don't know what she was telling the children.

Chapter 13: A Kidnapping.

Our neat home was transformed into a disordered house.

The living room was strewn with debris from the wreckage. Soledad packed for winter in Spain and temperate weather in Costa Rica. I stepped over the last-minute left-behind pieces of our life: clothes, toys, shoes and sandals, stuffed animals and baseball caps.

The bedrooms displayed the same carnage, with drawers left rifled and hanging open. The beds were unmade and rumpled covers mocked me, damp towels lay were the boys had dropped them in a rush. Large, opened, clear Tupperware storage containers with blue and purple lids stuck out from under the beds. In our bedroom, random pictures lay among the clothes and power cords, make-up and perfume bottles.

The kitchen sink held the plates that we had last used to eat. The forks and knives sat odd angles, a fly was stuck in syrup and a Sippy cup that last touched my daughter´s lips had now become garbage.

The basement toys were strewn about and the laundry was equally in shambles.

It looked like someone had come in, tossed the house, kidnapped whoever lived there and left on the run, like an abduction during a fire drill.

I didn't know it at the time, but I was standing in a crime scene, weeping, alone. The children had been kidnapped and I drove the get-away car to the airport.

The children would never come back to that life. I would never know that life again. My active role as a father ended that day; I just didn't know it until three years later. For purposes of self-preservation, I had the hope of a just-world to assuage the pain of my daily suffering.

I began the clean-up process and shed tears in earnest. Our life in that house died and was suddenly transformed into memories, things to be donated or garbage to be tossed in the bin for Friday morning pick-up.

Each room that I cleaned held the energy from my children. I sat crying on the basement steps next to the back door, looking at Ted's black cowboy boots, one standing upright and the other tipped on its side. He had been the last person to touch them and now he would never touch them again. The temptation was to leave their belongings where they lay, but that is a passing fancy of the defeated, exploring the depths of self-pity. I wasn't defeated.

Although powerless, I was a practical man.

I started cleaning up. I donated bags and bags of clothing. I donated toys by the box. Slowly sifting through every toy we had, separating with tears the toys that bore particular sentimental value. It was a profound process. I thought about parents whose children have died and how they go about the same process. Discarding the material possessions and with them, the memories of the children.

"Hail Mary, full of grace..."

Chapter 14: Christmas Fast.

Late November, winter and Thanksgiving on the doorstep and I was teaching high school Spanish and ESL in Philadelphia at Urban Academy Charter High School.

My wife sent me an email when she arrived in Spain. I had four weeks to wait until I flew to Spain for Christmas with my family. The gestating loss of my children was only in the first trimester, hints of the dramatic change to come were visceral pangs of emotional pain, like morning sickness that lasts all day. I would manage. I had no choice.

I had no contact number to call my sister-in-law in Spain. For three days my wife didn't return my emails. I called my mother-in-law for an explanation and assistance. The children were cut off from me.

I panicked but was reassured by my mother-in-law that she would get me the telephone number so I could call the children. The power game for a Voice in the Lives of our Children had begun without my knowledge. I was way late to the game; I stopped for gas and was out by the concession stands buying a hot dog for most of the first half, while my wife ran up the score: she was 5,000 miles away, she had the children, her next husband, a bank card and a letter from Domestic Violence Counseling. Her husband was living by fool's principles believing her lie of reconciliation.

Any influence as a father ended when that plane took off from New York, I just didn't know it.

Soledad called me and I talked to the boys and Elizabeth; I never got her sister's phone number. Communication was now completely under the control of my wife and has been ever since. The children and I were newly under the oppressive thumb of my wife, four years later and we still are.

I sent my wife an email asking for which date I should arrive and which airport I should fly into.

My wife contacted me through Yahoo Chat and told me not to come because there, "wasn't enough room for me." My wife has not made room for me in the lives of our children for four years now. That hasn't changed.

I felt the double barrel of the gun press up tight against my belly before the shotgun blast tore me inside out. I couldn't come to see the children at Christmas? I wouldn't see the children until Easter?

She said that she was being, "suffocated" by her sister.

She told me I wasn't helping and that I was suffocating her too. (She had a real suffocating problem that one.)

I wrote the following to her as a summary of that conversation:

"So, I don't have any means to call you or the children, I don't know the next time I will see or speak with you or the children. You are unclear about when you will return to Costa Rica and I have no say in your plans."

She responded: "You set up phone calls for Sunday so we will call you on Sunday."

"Ok" I typed. What else could I do? I cried. The emotional pain of loss and injustice was physically and mentally immobilizing.

This was turning into a kidnapping. I felt I had nothing to bargain with. My mother and father suggested I cut off funding. Cut-off her bank card and see how far she gets without money. Make her come back here. The classic Brute Irish tactics were beneath me at the time, but would later become my best option for seeing my children.

I couldn't employ an all-out act of war just yet and that goes against a basic Brute Irish premise that I learned in Life's Little Instruction Book: "When a fight is unavoidable, hit first and hit hard." My wife told me that we were reconciling and that she needed this time and that if I loved her and trusted her then it will work out for everyone's benefit.

I believed in my wife and my principles.

I am left with only principles.

"Dear Lord, Jesus Christ, have mercy on my soul."

*My custodial rights ended when Soledad refused to give me her sister's telephone number. I didn't understand why she wouldn't give me the number. I know now it was because she had moved in with Dan Knight.

When I did talk with the children, I could feel her presence in the back ground, hovering over the children as they spoke. I don't know how she manipulated the children to avoid any mention of Dan Knight's existence.

Chapter 15: 47 Days Until I See My Children?

Christmas of 2010 was the first Christmas our family spent apart. I didn't know that I would have to live with at least three more Christmases apart and as of this writing I see no future Christmases together. But at the time, I did what I could to survive.

I fasted for three days. I slept, read, watched movies and picked up smoking cigarettes, stepping outside into the cold every few hours to make sure I could still feel anything. I drank water and tea and ate small pieces of chocolate. My parents and sister and brothers called for me to come to dinner and all the events that surround Christmas.

There was no possibility of me sitting down without my children and watching other children enjoy Christmas; children in general only punctuated my loss. I cried passing the toy section of Wal-Mart; the exposed chubby legs of a baby destroyed me in the Acme; TV commercials with smiling kids tearing into gifts and hugging their parents put me on the floor.

I understand why the suicide rate increases during the holidays. The holidays exponentially increase the pain and exposure to our personal emptiness.

My children had been taken and with them went my identity. I had to begin reconstructing, piece by piece, some kind of life that was worth living. I couldn't kill myself. I had three children who were wondering where I was and who wanted a father. I could only learn to live with the pain.

"Hail Mary, full of grace, the Lord is with thee…"

Christmas passed.

I used our calendar in the kitchen and back counted the days until Easter Break. There were forty-seven days until I could fly to Costa Rica to be with the children.

I adjusted my calling plan and now had unlimited calling to Costa Rica. The children had arrived there and were living in my mother-in-law's house. I called every day.

The boys and I began counting the days. The first question from Ted or Sean would always be, "How many days left Papá?"

It was awkward living this life on the telephone. My wife spoke to me less and less and I could feel the undiminished hatred when she did speak.

Nothing had changed with her attitude towards me. I was being given no credit for the sacrifices and I began to curse Stephen Covey. I doubted my principles that had put me into this situation.

I had worked on practical man values of credit points for acts of valor and sacrifice. My practical approach, my logic, would betray me time and again until I learned to integrate my emotions with my actions.

Forty-seven days until I see my children. I can do it. Small achievable goals are the foundation of survival when faced with a seemingly impossible task.

"...Pray for us sinners..."

Chapter 16: Sidelined as a Father.

I called almost every day and in late January, when I asked to speak with my wife, she wasn't there. One of my mother-in-law's friends was watching the children. I remember thinking, "Great. Soledad is getting out." It was important to me that my wife engage in activities that were outside her role as a mother/wife. Mental health requires a rounded perspective says the practical man. Motherhood can crush other identities and overwhelm a person to the point of debilitation.

The next night when I called, Soledad was still not there and Maria (a friend of my mother-in-law) was watching the children.

The third night when she was not there I asked to speak with Maria. "Where is my wife?" I asked.

Maria admitted to me that Soledad was in the United States. She went there for a few days.

She was here? Why didn't she call? Why didn't she come to pick-up things the children could use? Why didn't she tell me?

I called my in-laws to ask about the situation. Vincent, my Italian-American father-in-law told me that he didn't know what Soledad was doing. He said that she didn't contact me because she was afraid.

Afraid of what? I didn't know. He didn't know either but that is what she said.

My wife had left our children in the hands of a stranger to them. Elizabeth was a year and 5 months old at the time and Soledad was willing to leave her.

The next night I called, my wife was in Costa Rica. She told me she didn't want to talk about it. I had no control over her actions. I asked her to reverse the situation and consider what she would think/feel/do if I had left our children with a stranger for four days?

It didn't matter. I had no influence, no control and no power. She said she was taking care of the children.

Or was she?

*Soledad had returned to the U.S. for an interview for her Citizenship. She wasn't going to let not residing in the United States affect getting her U.S. Citizenship.

She stayed with Dan Knight in NYC. He provided me with the airline ticket receipts and pictures of their time in NYC together.

Chapter 17: The Magic Cancer Powder.

In February, Sean was scheduled to have his cancer screening. He was supposed to have a urine test and blood samples.

Soledad told me she was handling this from Costa Rica but the tests from Costa Rica were unavailable or expensive. I suggested that she fly back to the U.S. with him and get his tests done.

She refused.

I had trouble conceptualizing her thought process.

Why would we not get our son tested for cancer? If Sean's cancer were to return the outcome is not good. If he is lucky it could be retinoblastoma, in which case doctors can pluck out that eye or the one where it gets ya' in the knees. They chop off the leg for that one.

One eyed or one legged is a victory for childhood cancer patients. In the land of the blind, the one eyed man is king and in the land of childhood cancer, the one legged boy is ALIVE!

I had excellent health benefits at the time.

Since Soledad flat out refused to return to have Sean tested, I contacted our Oncologist to see if time and temperature would have an effect on a urine sample. The Oncologist said if I ship the urine overnight, it would still be a valid sample. All Sean had to do was pee in a cup, I arranged for Fed Ex to collect the sample and Sean could be tested. Problem solved.

I thought.

Soledad refused. She asked me, "Why are you doing this?

I had the same question for her. She didn't answer mine and Practical John answered, "Because we have a son who is in remission from cancer...blah blah blah..."

The only explanation I could figure out from the lies she was telling me was that my wife wasn't mentally well.

She would say she is protecting family.

From what was she protecting our children? What is the collateral damage of her "protecting" our children? How much emotional pain have my children suffered from the separation of their father, their home and the unknowing of an uncertain future where they are denied access to their father?

"I was protecting my family," is the mantra of every abducting parent who ever stole a kid.

I called her father to appeal to his reason and found none.

I asked him, "Why would we not have Sean pee in a cup and test his urine according to his treatment schedule?"

He said, "You could put something in the sample that would give Sean a positive result and force Soledad to return to the U.S."

I never thought of forcing her to stay. I had already let her go twice. I didn't even know we were in an adversarial relationship. I thought we were two oxen still pulling the same plow.

What did my wife think?

I would be playing catch-up to her thought process for years until I gave up trying to apply logic to her thought process. Once I stopped trying to catch-up, she turned around and started walking back towards me. That process would take me three years to achieve. At the time, I was just learning that I had certainly become the enemy.

If my wife thought I was willing to "trap" her, her thoughts were distant from mine. What was she willing to do?

I am still amazed to find out.

We were speaking in Spanish and I couldn't believe my father-in-law's logic. I repeated what he said, so I was certain that I wasn't confused. I refrained from sarcasm and my natural instinct to say, "So you think I have the magic cancer powder to put into Sean's urine? You think I hold this one amino acid that indicates a return of cancerous cells?"

My father-in-law, a zealous bible banger told me, "Sean is cured." "God has cured him."

So that had to be good enough for me.

I did not argue. I expressed my disagreement but refrained from letting him know exactly what I thought of his logic. I was talking to someone on another plane. Reasoning and logic were of no consequence and I didn't need to openly declare war with him. I didn't need any more enemies.

"Holy Mary, mother of God, pray for us sinners…"

I hung-up the phone and thought about what my wife was willing to risk to keep the children from returning to the U.S. Reconciliation seemed far afield from her intentions. I was beginning to realize that I was out. I now had no power to influence the health choices my wife was making for our children and most specifically those for Sean, a childhood cancer survivor.

I thought about the situation and wrote an email to my wife.

I told her that I spoke to her father. I told her his theory about the magic cancer powder that I could potentially introduce to Sean's urine sample. I offered to have the urine sample sent to my mother-in-law's U.S. address. She could take the sample to Children's Hospital of Philadelphia and I would never have to touch it. I could provide transportation for my mother-in-law if that was a problem for her.

Soledad refused.

I was stunned beyond words. I was willing to let my wife go but I could not fathom the logic of not having Sean tested in Philadelphia at a time when he was medically insured. Costa Rica could not provide the technology for childhood cancer that was available in the U.S. If Sean's health had relied on the Costa Rican Medical System he would be dead.

My son would remain untested. Appeals to my wife, my mother-in-law, my father-in-law and my sister-in-law fell on deaf ears.

What my wife was willing to risk to remove me from the lives of our children goes far beyond what I considered in the best interest of our children. To date I fail to comprehend the decision making process of the woman who gave birth to our children.

"...pray for us sinners, now and at the hour of our death. Amen."

Chapter 18: Counting the Days.

Sean and Ted and I continued to count the days until I arrived in Costa Rica. I called at least five times a week and each night Ted would likely answer the phone. The first words out of his mouth: "Papá, I knew it was you." I have a connection with Ted on a spiritual level that transcends words and place and time. He felt my energy in the ringtone; he felt my energy from afar, calling to him, reaching out to him.

When my wife would get on the phone her tone was not so enthusiastic. She was done with me intruding on her life, I didn't know it at the time, but that is what was happening.

I was no longer a father, I was an intrusion.

With 21 days until I arrived in Costa Rica to visit my family for Semana Santa (Easter Week), I received a Divorce Proposal.

It fell from the sky like debris from a plane explosion; it dwarfed my being and crushed my spirit. When I read it my feelings were void.

I didn't even know we were getting a divorce.

My wife requested supervised visits with our children. What? Huh? When did my ability as a father come into play? Sure, she didn't love me and couldn't support my presence but now the children were being sequestered. She wanted me in Anger Management Classes and to take monthly drug tests.

My wife requested $1,800 a month for Child Support. As a teacher in Costa Rica, I would be lucky to bring home $1,000 dollars a month.

She wanted the house in Costa Rica and I could keep the Bensalem house. It didn't seem all that fair, nor even realistic.

I consulted my friend Don Roberto who is a kind man and a great thinker. He is a guide and an advisor in my life and a lawyer in Costa Rica.

I forwarded him the divorce proposal and told him of my plans to visit at Easter. He was clear on one thing: Do not enter Costa Rica.

He explained that if I enter the country, my wife could file for Child Support and then I would not be permitted to leave the country until the courts arrived at a decision. I would either have to sign and agree to what she wanted OR remain in Costa Rica to negotiate and thus lose my job as a teacher in the U.S.

There existed a third possibility which we didn't discuss but which would ultimately be my best option: illegally exit Costa Rica by means of highways and byways and bribes.

I spoke with Soledad. She told me to sign the papers. I spoke with my mother-in-law, she said, "Sign the papers."

I explained how a visit with the children had nothing to do with the divorce. How can she hold the unfair divorce proposal over my head and dangle the visit with our children. It just did not make any moral sense to my mind.

Don't involve the children in a Divorce is a moral truth. I am principled against any such unfair action…who isn't? Some people live by, "All is fair in love and war."

I went to a lawyer in Pennsylvania.

Chapter 19: Late to the Party.

The office was located in a posh area of Historic Bucks County in a 150 year old house on the Historic Registry.

The sharp looking lawyer got the abridged version of our financials and what my wife was demanding.

He was a 50ish Brooks Brother suspender wearing lawyer, but still a meat and potatoes guy, big and well-pressed with the confidence of age and money. He listened and took a few notes.

I then went into how my wife was painting me: drug addicted, abusive, alcoholic, knife carrying, gay, porn addicted, controlling, violent, rapist. He didn't blink at the tale. He had heard it all before. He stopped me short and summarized my situation with few words:

"So she believes her own bullshit."

That articulates the nature of her allegations.

He laid it out. Soledad was entitled to the appreciation on both houses but none of the principle. When he calculated how much I made a month and a minimum that my wife could make monthly, he rounded the child support at about $900 a month…call it a grand.

She married a teacher and we had three kids and were just starting our lives. We had only accumulated debt since living in the United States.

Then the lawyer sat back in his chair and made a steeple with his fingers. This story sounded familiar. He pushed a button on the desk phone and asked me my wife's name again. He told his Secretary: Check on files for a Soledad Negro.

It was late March and spring was peeking through the windows as afternoon sunlight slanted through the blinds. We sat for a moment and then the intercom came back to life and the secretary said she had the file. "Please bring it in."

The previous October, when I was grasping for straws to find the Make My Wife Happy Straw, she was meeting with this very same lawyer about divorcing me and he was saying the same thing to her: You don't get either of the houses and it is about $900 a month in child support."

What are the odds of us both going to the same lawyer? Thanks to his prime location in the Google line-up and his upscale address, the odds were pretty darn good.

"Well, that's a first for me and I've been practicing for 25 years," and he stood to shake my hand.

"So, good luck, but I can't represent you. I'll send you an email recommending a friend of mine. Be very careful, it looks like you are late to the party and that is never good."

It was during this time that I made a brief switch to the "Our Father" as my prayer of choice.

"Forgive us our trespasses, as we forgive those who trespass against us..."

* Soledad had been committed to Dan Knight for over a year at this point.

Chapter 20: Tears.

We still needed money, essentially more money since I was supporting two households and things just aren't so cheap in Costa Rica. We had free school here and now we were paying for schools there and gas is four bucks a gallon in Costa Rica.

I got a second job as an online teacher, developed my business model for Flat World Educators, designed and published my website, but most importantly, I began writing in earnest, what I thought were clever stories of my experiences as an international educator with tales of Cairo and the Caribbean.

I was flush with free time and used it all to improve my life and occupy my mind, to be ready for when I was able to be father to my children once again.

My wife had her own bank card and she withdrew money as she saw fit. She was managing three children on her own. That was no way easy. It is a daunting task but yet one she chose. She would rather do everything than have me do anything (aside from providing moolah).

Easter approached slowly. We counted the days and I cried throughout the day: Driving to work I sopped tissues, every day at school I stepped into the hallway or the bathroom to cry, at lunch, alone in my room, I wept openly. Driving home I welled up knowing the house was silent and empty. Entering the house I let them flow.

For the nightly phone call to Sean, Ted and Elizabeth, I would steel myself to achieve only one goal while speaking with them: Do Not Cry Aloud.

I was selfish with my fear and pain. Why expose my children, so young in their lives, to the deep suffering and vulnerability of the human condition; to crumble the image of father as protector? They don't need to hear their father brought so low, that time will come, but please not yet.

I was successful some nights, other nights, not so much. I spoke little and listened more, then swung the mouthpiece skyward and cupped my hand down over my own mouth, gasping. Salt and sweat and tears ran over my clenched fingers…one deep breath and then… "Okay Sean, I will give you a call tomorrow night. I love you very much."

And I hang up. I hit the floor as crumpled dead weight and the tears hit the floor all but silently. I can still see the transparent circles of my tears, magnifying the fake grain of Pergo flooring. I can still hear the soft sound from the slow but steady stream of saltwater falling on laminate: "pat… pat… pat…" barely audible from my horizontal position, but no less real, like the faint sound of a cat walking.

I lived that for six months straight.

"Hail Mary…full of grace, the Lord is with thee…"

Chapter 21: I Don't Know…

It was Thursday before Easter Break and my flight to Costa Rica was scheduled for Saturday. I was still unsure about entering Costa Rica. My legal counsel told me in no uncertain terms, "Do not go to Costa Rica unless you are prepared to leave your job and home and remain in Costa Rica for at least 6 months."

I continued to speak with the children on the telephone and we counted the days, although my hope of seeing them had turned anemic.

My wife's answer to any question about visiting was, "Sign the divorce." Finally, she acquiesced and gave me an answer to my question: "If I come, will you allow me to see the children?" She answered: "I don't know."

She doesn't know, oh well, alright then. She doesn't know if she will allow me to see our children and my flight is in two days, a new low for me and her and the children.

I decided that I couldn't take the risk.

My wife said to me, "Just forget about us and finish your doctoral degree."

"Just forget." That was not possible. I can't forget my children. They are a part of me. They comprise my identity and my love and my core beliefs: be a father. Spend time with your children. Nothing is more valuable than time invested in children. I am an educator and everything in life is education for me. It is my lens. That lens focuses on children and their intellectual, social and emotional development.

Saturday came, my flight went and I stayed.

"Our Father, who art in heaven…"

I untacked the calendar from the kitchen wall and counted from my last day of school at Urban Academy Charter High School. I finished on Friday, 23 June and would be on a plane the following day.

I started on 24 June and wrote the number one. When I arrived to that Saturday in April the number was 74. I would empty the house, rent it and move to Costa Rica to be with my children. Everything would be better once I was re-established in their lives. She could not keep me from them. I thought. Fool of fools, I then was.

I spoke with the boys and told them of the new countdown date. I promised Ted that I would never be away from them for this long again. I was proven wrong and broke that promise too. The idea that my wife, with the help of the courts, would allow my children to be cut off from me did not even enter my mind. No justice system would permit it. I was faultless, I thought.

My wife got on the phone a few days later and piled on. She asked, "How could you do this to Ted? You don't want to come and see him. You don't even care to see your children."

What was this woman talking about? After pointing the Divorce Proposal like a gun she has altered my response from: "I don't think that is a fair Divorce Proposal, please allow me to come and see the children," to, "Your father doesn't want to see you."

Ted thinks I didn't want to see him?

I know that ya' can't win in life. I ain't even lookin' to win but a little bit of justice is a fair expectation. Justice would not visit me for years. Justice is a blind old bat wandering the streets and she sure as shit isn't lookin' for me. I banged big gongs for Justice to come but I ultimately ended up in a shite state of affairs. No matter which choice I make, my wife will be certain to interpret my actions as nefarious. It is a self-defense mechanism of the righteous.

What I do or not is of little consequence to her story.

Chapter 22: Soledad's Prediction.

Near Easter in 2010, I was in my Bensalem bedroom on the telephone with my wife in Costa Rica. It was about 8:15pm and dark outside. My wife told me that she was considering a job in California. I told her, "No way." She chose Costa Rica and I was coming to Costa Rica. I did not like the idea of chasing my wife around the world and playing catch-up with my career for her every whim. She chose Costa Rica and I would be there in June.

She realized that she was stuck in Costa Rica. I told her I would refuse to sign the documents that would allow her to take the children out of Costa Rica. If one parent refuses, the children cannot leave the country. This is a fair safeguard to protect children from parental abduction and in this case the law would work in my favor.

At least I could keep her in Costa Rica. I got burnt allowing her to leave the U.S. and that wouldn't happen again.

When I was nine, my baseball coach said, "Fool me once, shame on you. Fool me twice, shame on me." My blind faith in my principles and values and the perfection of the universe, has at times, opened me up to hard knocks, where and I am forced to learn by egg-on-face experience.

But I wasn't going to let her fool me twice.

She responded, "Your parents will never see the children again."

I was unwittingly in a bare knuckle street fight, pushed to the center of a dark ring before any lights came-on. I knew nothing about the rules of conduct. There were no rules. Cover yer balls and prepare yourself for severe biting and ruthless eye gouging. Unprepared, I took a beating from passive resistance. On the violent ground, I suffered the boot falls from those whom I expected either love or justice; I can still smell the faint odor of gun oil and shoe polish left on the hair in my nostrils. One derelict question was set adrift that night on the sea of my mind.

Would my children ever see my parent's again?

Chapter 23: Elizabeth.

The day the plan took off with my children I began writing a diary to them, to stand as testament to what I did and how I felt and thought at any given time since our forced separation.

Below is an entry:

26 April 2011

My dearest Children,

Oh, the joy!
Today Sean, you gave the phone to Elizabeth and helped her say, "Papá."

I am so proud of you. This is the concept of family that I hope to instill in each of you. Family helps each other. We help each other to find our happiness.
You helped and she gained from your help and I have felt the utter joy from hearing her voice.

I Love you Dearly,
Papá

The connection I felt towards Elizabeth and Sean after this conversation reassured me that my children were functioning with me in mind although I was not there in body. I called about every night for those months when I was in the U.S. and the children were in Costa Rica.

Elizabeth was just learning to speak and the word that my son chose to teach her: Papá.

God Bless Sean.

Another journal entry looks like this:

6 May 2011

My Dear Elizabeth,

Tonight we spoke for 17 minutes and 23 seconds.

You are 1 year, 7 months and 26 days old.

We talked and talked. I sang. You said, "Papá" three times. You also knew the words, "Silly" and "Sean."

I told you how much I miss you, how much I love you. How beautiful you are. I told you that I would dance at your wedding.

I told you my dreams and you told me yours.

You answered the phone. I didn't speak with Ted or Sean.

It was only you My Love. My God. I adore you.

- Papá

Elizabeth was used to the phone calls and the boys picking-up the phone every night. She wanted in and she wanted to speak with Papá. She had only a three word vocabulary but she understood the voice inflection of conversation.

The conversation had questions and answers, "Blah blah blah blah Sean."

To which I would respond, "Yes, my love, Sean is a good brother. I think about you every day. I'll see you soon."

And off Elizabeth would go again using baby talk and her three words: Sean, Papá and Silly.

We kept that conversation going for more than 15 minutes of pure joy in communication while I sat in our living room looking at our family pictures.

I was taken from her life long before she was able to retain memories of me and it is this pain that wakes me in the night. It is this pain that makes me question God and his designs. How and why does my daughter, the wavy haired beauty, not know her father?

* On May 26, Soledad flies to Oregon and leaves the children in Costa Rica for eleven days. Dan Knight and Soledad drive across country and on June 6, she flies from NYC to Costa Rica. Dan Knight provided airline itinerary receipts and pictures of their cross country trip.

"Thy kingdom come, Thy will be done…"

Chapter 24: Communication Severed.

The Children and I counted down the days from 74. The number was above their ability to conceptualize but as the numbers grew more familiar our excitement grew likewise. We practiced the names of the months. From April to May and then June…fifteen days…ten days and we were all electric with excitement, except my wife.

Five days left…on day number four, I called in the evening: there was no answer, the phone rang unattended. With three days left the phone rang and rang…two days left and no answer. I was now officially cut off from speaking with my children.

I stripped the house bare and rented it to kind people. My family and some friends came to the house on Friday and we all worked into the night packing dishes and shuffling everything into the attic and dragging the rest to the curb.

I finished school on Friday and left for Costa Rica on Saturday. The cleaning wasn't done when I left, but my brothers and sister came the next two days and continued to clean. God Bless my family.

I arrived in Costa Rica, rented a car and drove to my friend Steve's store. As advised by counsel, he came with me to my mother-in-law's house so I would have a witness to the reunion with my children. My family had fallen so far down the rabbit hole, with communication so far lost, that I needed witnesses to attest to the events in my life.

My life had reached a new low, but had not nearly settled on rock bottom, in fact, fathoms of emotional pain awaited me. Emotional pain is a wasted experience without self-reflection to identify the causes and accept responsibility. From these reflective practices comes emotional growth and his cousin spiritual growth. Emotional pain is a "growing pain." I was in a free fall of emotional pain that would continue-on for a year and a half until I smuggled myself up a foggy mountain road to a lesser known, unprotected border crossing and found salvation, not from the courts or my wife but from within. I found the confidence to free myself from the judgment of others.

I spent three years seeking salvation from my wife, her family, our friends, lawyers and the Costa Rican Justice System, but the only measure of emotional growth came when I accepted the responsibility of my own salvation. I am my own judge and savior and no one else. I no longer relied on systems and others nor sought their approval: The need I had since childhood with nuns and parents and the carrot and the stick…over. I no longer bothered if anyone approved of me and my actions. I became my own man, but for the time in June 2011, when I arrived in Costa Rica to see my children, I was an approval seeking marionette on strings, dancing to the beat of a malicious puppeteer.

The door to my mother-in-law's house, where my wife and children lived, was closed. The car was in the driveway. I stood outside the 10 foot iron bar security fence and waited but no one came.

Steve and I walked down the street to Soledad's Grandparents' house. Abuelo (grandfather) and I kissed and I took a knee so Abuela (grandmother) could see and hear me better. At 88 years old, she was spending more and more time in the chair in the bedroom.

They received me with love. I had earned their respect over time and had developed a strong bond with Abuelo in particular. He had no news about where my family was and we left it at that. Although they lived one block from my wife and children, he said he didn't see them much. I told him that would change. I would bring the children around so they could know their great-grandfather. We hugged and kissed farewell, but not good-bye.

Steve and I went to my father-in-law's house about ten minutes away in a neighborhood called, Tibas. I tapped with a coin on the outside iron gate that separates the street and criminals from the driveway and the house. They live in an area where they need three rows of looping razor wire above their ten foot fence because two rows of prison style razor wire just weren't enough. Juana, my father-in-law's wife, came to the door. She peered through the security gate at the front door and the boys came running behind her.

Sean and Ted screamed and screamed with all their voice and emotion: "Papá! Papá! Papá!" They were electric.

Juana came out to the far gate where Steve and I stood in the street and she said that Soledad told her that if I came, I was not allowed to see the boys. She said that since they were screaming for me she would let me in to visit for a little while. That was the last act of common sense that I would witness from my wife's family, from there on out, I was the enemy, foul and evil, to be reviled, despised and kept at bay at all costs.

I thanked her and praised God and was reunited with Sean and Ted. We hugged and hugged and couldn't get enough of the physical contact that we had missed over the past six months.

Ted sat on my lap and Sean squeezed as close as he could to me on the couch. He wrapped his arms around me and I cried.

The mind can handle situations much better when we are psychologically prepared for an experience. A week before, I had told the boys that I would cry when I saw them and that they would be tears of joy. There is no shame in crying. I would share my joy but could not yet share the pain.

After twenty minutes of visiting and nothing but full hugging contact with Sean and Ted, my father-in-law arrived. He coldly received me and would have been less courteous if my friend Steve had not been by my side. Steve knows my father-in-law and they respect each other.

I assumed that I would meet with Soledad and we would arrange for me to visit with the children and most likely begin Divorce Proceedings. I did not want to appear pushy with my in-laws and after twenty-five minutes, I told the boys that I would leave in ten minutes and that I would be back to see them in the morning and that everything was going back to having me in their lives.

I was so wrong. It was like I was telling the boys lies, but at the time I knew no better. I really thought I would be allowed to see them and be their father. I was ignorant of the process in Costa Rica and equally unprepared for the measures my wife was willing to take to alienate me from my children. My ability to parent had never been questioned when the boys and I spent every waking minute together. That my wife didn't love me now morphed into, "He is a dangerous man and I have to protect my children from him." That is the mantra of bullshit excuses people use to justify all kinds of selfish actions.

Juana, my father-in-law's wife, told me that I was harming the boys by crying. She was angry. I explained that I had spoken with the boys beforehand and that these were tears of joy.

I had to exercise extreme caution when interacting with my wife, in-laws, clerks, judges, and lawyers, anyone who had some influence over my ability to see my children. If I wasn't emotionless and passive, I was considered aggressive and out of control.

So folk could poke at me and any sign of defense was an opportunity to be accused of losing my temper. I had such a visceral reaction to what I felt was the kidnapping of my children. I felt strongly about this situation but had to suppress urgency, emotion, fear and disagreement.

My father-in-law followed Steve and I to the outside fence and he told me that it was terrible to see Ted so afraid of me. My head always spun when I talked with this guy. I remained totally deadpan with him and said, "You really think that little boy was afraid of me? The one who didn't get up from my lap for the past 35 minutes?"

"Si, los dos tienen miedo a usted." "Yes, they are both afraid of you."

There was no doubt that my father-in-law believed my wife's bullshit too.

I asked Steve to check-in with reality: "Do you think they were afraid of me?"

"No way John." He asked my father-in-law, "De verdad pienses que los chiquitos tenian medio?" "Do you really think the children were afraid?"

"Si," said the man who thinks I have the magic cancer powder and am prepared to use it.

"Okay then, I will come by tomorrow morning at 10am to see the boys again."

Steve and I left and we knew that this was not going to end well. Steve looked on the bright side and said, "Hey, at least they let you in the door. As long as people open the door for you, there is some hope."

The doors would close the next day and remain closed for four years as of this writing.

The "could haves" and "would haves" haunt me. I could have tried to take the children with me then…but I didn't know any better. I was a teacher and principal with a clean record. I believed in justice. I believed that the system was plum and if I deviated from the law and took off my white hat, I would be subject to reproach. I thought I stood, at that time, beyond reproach.

No one is beyond reproach if there is a willing liar at the ready. (Read: <u>A Man for All Season's</u>.) My father believed liars are the most dangerous of enemies: "You can watch a thief, but you can't watch a liar." They kill from afar like a sniper firing a headshot from a mile away. You don't even hear the report of the rifle.

Liars and their lies are silent killers.

"The Lord is with thee, blessed art thou among…"

Chapter 25: Go Away.

My father-in-law is a candidate for Hoarders if that show ever goes international. The back room that used to be a porch is filled with old washers and TVs, cardboard boxes of fabric and tools, tiny live birds in rusted cages kick feed and poop on the floor amid flourishing plants living on the fine touch of Juana. She has a spectacular green thumb.

There is a second bathroom at the back of the house but that is filled with stuff so it is more like a full closet with a dry toilet. The back bedroom is filled with 60 wedding dresses that Soledad and I bought to start her business. They are a moldy testament to wasted time and money.

The following morning, when Steve and I arrived at 10am, the boys were in their pajamas. We hugged and kissed and felt each other close. I could smell the familiar scent of their warm sleep and I breathed it in deep to never forget it. There was a sense that life was changing for the better. It was a false sense.

I stayed for only ten minutes so as not to push my father-in-law. I told the boys I would be back in the afternoon to see them. We left with hugs and kisses and I still thought I was their father with all the rights and privileges to follow that role. After that meeting I would not see or speak with my children for 10 months. I thought I would see them in the afternoon and my wife and I could work out an arrangement for how we were going to live as a family.

She was clear about hating me as a husband but she never said she didn't want me to be a father to my children.

Steve and I went to my mother-in-law's house and knocked on the door. I still had not seen my girl Elizabeth. I was hoping Soledad was prepared to have a conversation about how we were to manage as two adults with the best interest of our children in mind.

No one answered the door.

I dropped Steve at work and spent the day in the city. I bought notebooks and pencils and a calendar for the boys. I wanted them to start writing journals or using picture journals to express themselves. I could see that my contact with them was going to be hindered by my wife. I could never have imagined how much so, but at this point I was on the threshold of knowledge, knocking on the door of enlightenment, but still outside, under the dim porch light of ignorance.

In the late afternoon, I returned to my father-in-law's house and tapped on the bars where my children had been imprisoned. No one answered and no one was home. The prisoners had been transferred.

I went to my mother-in-law's house and knocked. No answer.

I drove around the block looking for houses to rent. My idea was to rent a house in the same neighborhood so the children could come and go as they pleased. When I doubled back and passed the house, Soledad was coming out the door.

I got out of the car and she said two words, "Go away."

I raised my hand to wave and when I heard those words I said, "Okay," and got back in my car and drove away.

I had no witnesses with me. I did not want her to call the police. I thought if I played fair that my efforts would be rewarded. Life does not work that way in the short run. Life takes time to pay it forward. I waited over two years before I even began to see how my efforts would be rewarded with love and compassion, but not from my wife.

I suffered greatly in the meantime.

"Blessed art thou among women…"

Chapter 26: First Lawyer.

She was recommended by Don Roberto. He had guided me as a friend and a lawyer for the past several months and if he said she was his first choice, I had complete confidence in her. Again, I was so wrong. It seems that each decision I made was another stumbling block in achieving my goal.

Her name was Ivanna Grande Sinmorales, but the only things grand were her physical size and her avarice. The office building was shining and sleek with lots of light and clean lines with modern furniture. The secretary offered me a cappuccino which I accepted.

Her office was purple and pink and gaudy with big fake flowers and art-work she bought at Marshalls and a crap Erte from her coked up 70's disco days. There were unlit candles collecting dust on garish lacquered side stands. In place of a file cabinet, piles of paper, begging for a home, were strewn on the floor behind her glass topped desk.

She wasn't so good with email and she didn't know how to text. Still, I had faith.

She told me how she had friends in the courts and that some judges had been her students. She was in her early fifties and squeezed herself into business suits too tight for professional wear. She had the anger of a chubby lesbian vegan.

The first step is to request Provisional Visitation. Her total cost for the procedure in Family Court was $3,000. She wanted a deposit and I paid her half the fee. I had the cash on me. "Better to pay up front than run short later on," I reasoned erroneously.

I know now it is better to pay the least amount you can up front to keep the incentive alive. I applied that lesson a year and a half later when I bribed immigration officials at the border.

I left the office confident with her efforts and my clean record that the justice system would be fair and swift. She suggested that the Family Court Visitation process would take three months. Either she was lying to me or she didn't know anything about the system. She already knew the position my wife's lawyer was taking: stall.

Both my wife's lawyer and Ms. Sinmorales were playing phone tag and both refused to make the next move. It was a pissing contest between two family lawyers in Costa Rica. Sinmorales refused to call again, so there was no communication. This is an indicator for an extended court process or more accurately, an infinitum court process. When I asked my lawyer to continue efforts to communicate, she flat out refused.

I can tell you now, that the process can take over two years. Easy. A woman can hold onto the children for two years without even breaking a sweat. No phone calls, don't visit the school. The best you can hope for are six supervised visits in the courthouse: five hours in two years. That's it.

Two weeks after our initial meeting, Sinmorales received the Provisional Visitation documents. I was granted visits every Saturday from 9-5. It was at least something. It meant contact with my children. I could live with that. I now had hope to see my children in the coming three weeks.

Ms. Sinmorales received the document on a Thursday and she told me it would be unlikely that my wife could be notified by the weekend but by the following week we could get her notified. The law states that she needs to be notified by hand: no emails to her lawyer or any kind of 21st century communication tactics: hand delivered is the only way in a country that has zero neighborhood street signs and no numerical addresses.

I told Ms. Sinmorales that I would pay to expedite the process. If we had to pay off a delivery guy down at the courthouse I was not above some baksheesh to make this happen.

The following week my wife still had not been notified. I spoke with an associate at Sinmorales' law firm who told me they had not been able to notify Soledad. I told him I didn't want to hear about the reasons he couldn't notify her. I wanted results. Put someone at her door and wait. It is easy. Make it happen.

I wanted to see my children so badly, the pain was bleeding me. Just that week I called my mother-in-law's house where my wife and the children lived. Sean answered the phone. He said four words before my wife took the receiver from him. These words echo the uncertainty that my children were experiencing.

He said: "Papá, where are you?"

My wife told me never to call there again. Click.

I spoke with Sinmorales on the telephone on Friday. She had not returned my calls the previous days. She said that she didn't remember telling me that my wife would be notified by this week and that she couldn't keep track of every conversation she had. She then said I was, "too demanding" a client and that she didn't want to work for me.

"Please wait," I said. "I am not interested in you quitting. What I am hoping is that we can effectively communicate." "No" she said, she didn't want to work with me.

She was also keeping all of my money. The one document that she filed should have cost me $400 at the most. Lawyer fees are capped in Costa Rica. There is a standard fee that can be applied and it tops at $400. I had paid $1,500 for my one filing. She kept the money and quit.

I appealed to Don Roberto to intervene. I couldn't afford to lose half of my attorney money in the first two weeks in the country.

After Don Roberto spoke with Sinmorales he told me that I, "raised my voice" to her associate. He then advised me to not pursue the money because Sinmorales could go to my wife's lawyer and say that I had, "raised my voice," and that it was clear that I had an Anger Management problem and that I was aggressive. Sinmorales could say she was afraid of me and that would not bode well for my case.

I was learning the ways. Although I could easily rave up and down the walls about my pain and anguish, if I did so, I would undermine my case. I needed to remain completely passive although my children were abducted from me and that the last words I heard from my son were: Where are you?

I wonder if I were a woman and I cried and yelled and screamed in the halls of justice that my husband had taken my children…would people identify that reaction as "motherly" and "natural?" I would.

Don Roberto didn't know nothing about all that. He gave me sound advice: "Keep your mouth shut and take it." I made an amendment to the policy:

Get used to it.

My children had been abducted. I was now being worked by a system that did not recognize my rights nor have the least bit of interest in moving the process forward at less than a glacial pace. My children's rights were also being ignored. How did they feel? What did they think about their father? What was my wife telling them?

I am a teacher, I lived and breathed for the time with my children and now that they were taken from me I was supposed to be meek and passive and quiet. I wanted to take down the courthouse with a sledgehammer.

My children were stolen. I'll burn down the world to get them back.

I was being sodomized and I could do nothing but quietly accept. It was the beginning of a jailhouse train on the fresh fish that each big dog in the system was running on me. The hole torn into me by my wife was now being ripped larger by the players in the justice system. Everybody was getting a piece and the slow bleed started. I collapsed in the shower, and blood mixing with water ran down the drain.

I prayed and prayed. As soon as my eyes opened in the morning and the last moments in the night, I distracted my mind with prayer.

* On 6 July, Soledad leaves the children in Costa Rica for ten days and travels to NYC to visit Dan Knight and complete her Citizenship Process. She legally becomes a U.S. Citizen. Dan Knight has provided photos and airlines receipts confirming this information.

"Holy Mary, Mother of God, pray for us sinners…"

Chapter 27: Lawyer Number Two.

Lawyer number two was again recommended by my friend Don Roberto. Lawyer Number Two was a guy in his early fifties. He had an office in a sharp house in a semi-plush neighborhood. Paintings of traditional Costa Rican handcarts and typical Tico Houses lined the walls. The wooden conference room was dark and ominous.

Costa Rican lawyers are accustomed to people acquiescing. They are the super snobs of Costa Rica. This lawyer was no different; he didn't consider us in the same intellectual league. He wanted to ask me questions but didn't want to answer mine. It was like I was supposed to be impressed with the office and intimidated by his choice of neckwear.

He laid out the plan and said he couldn't promise anything. He gave me no timetable but said it could take 3 months, 6 months or two years. He had seen cases run long, depending on how aggressive the opposing party wants to be. He was vaguely honest, so I could tolerate his being condescending.

It would cost $400 to file our next paperwork but we had to get my wife notified of the Provisional Visitation that the judge ordered. Until she was notified, we were in a holding pattern.

I called this guy once a week and he told me that my wife had not yet been notified and he told me not to call anymore, that he would call me when she was notified. Does anyone realize that I am losing days and weeks in the lives of my children? It sure felt like abduction: I could neither see nor speak with Elizabeth, Ted and Sean.

Since lawyers are paid piecemeal and only for what they file, they do not want to hear from the client until the paperwork clears, then they can schedule another meeting and file another paper and collect more money. Any emails or phone contact in the meantime are a waste of time and loss of money. They get paid to write and file paperwork, not to discuss the case or push.

Six weeks passed and my wife had not been notified. I went to the First Circuit Family Court in San Jose. I had my passport and case number and all the eyes downward humility/meekness I could feign. I wanted to scream at the top of my lungs that my children had been abducted. I wanted to lie on the floor and cry to express the pain. "I want to talk to my children!"

I asked to see the case and the young clerk handed over the documents. The Provisional Visitation Document was on top. My wife had not been notified. I showed the clerk the dates and asked how can I get my wife notified. She read the docs and told me they tried to notify my wife but she didn't answer the door so they sent the documents back to the Family Court office for review.

"Ok, then how do we get her notified? I haven't seen my children in 6 weeks waiting for this document to get into her hands."

"Oh, I have to send it back upstairs."

"Ok, when can you send that document back upstairs?"

"I think I can get to it today."

Next question: "Where are you sending it to?"

"It goes to the Office of Communication on the third floor."

"Thank you so much. I really appreciate your time and God Bless."

Next Day: I return to the San Jose Courthouse and climb the steps to the third floor and look for the Communications Office. I asked the kind girl to please see if my documents have arrived to their office. I explained that I had not seen or spoken with my children in six weeks.

What I didn't know was how utterly common my story was. Kids go years with their fathers taken out of the picture, so six weeks was nothing to the folk in these hallways and offices.

What I did get from this girl was answers. The office of communications was excellent and in general the people I dealt with for a year and a half in the Costa Rican Court System tried to help me. Unfortunately, each felt as strapped down by the system as me, so they wash their hands like Pilate and wait for the next coffee break.

She told me the courier had twice been to my mother-in-law's house where my wife and children were living, but both times no one answered the door. On one report it stated that the lights were on and the white Toyota of such and such a license number was in the driveway but nobody answered the door.

I asked the girl what happens if the person doesn't answer the door. She said that can go on for months or longer and some people never get notified and the proceedings never move forward.

I had a glimpse of this in the past and it jumped to the forefront of my mind. My wife's former boss had a Demand against her for their undefined business arrangements. She told me at the time that it was no big deal and as long as you don't answer the door for the delivery person, nothing ever happens. It is a stall technique that is very effective because that delivery guy who makes minimum wage doesn't really want to have to wait around to deliver a piece of paper that is meaningless to him. He knocks once and moves on with his deliveries.

Now I was on the stinky end of this, "avoid the notification tactic." My children and I were losing time together because of the susceptibility of the system to abuse without restraint or reprimand.

I asked the young female clerk when the next time the notification would be attempted. She told me that Moses (I had faith in Moses), was scheduled to try and notify my wife in the afternoon. I was thrilled. "How can I check to see if she has been notified?" I asked.

The clerk gave me the direct number to the Communications Office and told me I could call the next morning.

The next morning I called and my wife had been notified. The wheels where turning. I just had to find another lawyer.

Chapter 28: Moving the Papers.

How is it that I could get my wife notified in two days when two seasoned lawyers couldn't get it done in six weeks?
Simple: My lawyers didn't give a shite.
I was a cog in the machine. Costa Rican lawyers have no interest in pushing the government offices to move. They need to work with those offices on a regular basis, so they try not to make any waves.

If they get known to be trouble makers, then their chances of getting a judgeship down the road will be jeopardized. If the judges don't like them, the lawyers *feel* they will never get a judgment in their favor. The lawyers suck the brown eye of any judge and low level clerk in the building and advocating for the clients comes in very near the end of the race and far behind cashing the checks.

My high priced, expensive tied lawyer was just going to sit while that paper sat, in the wrong office, until somebody moved the wheels and showed they cared. Nobody cared that the, "Provisional Visitation Rights" for the Murphy children sat lifeless in a drawer.

This was the document that held the key to my children having a father and it meant nothing to anyone except me.

I helped move that document from the first to the third floor and from the third floor to my wife's hands in two days. I was learning the system.

Whether that lawyer didn't know enough to move the doc or didn't care enough, either way, he was absolutely useless to me and my children.

I thought, "Even folk that I am paying are dragging their feet."

I wanted to express what I was willing to do, so I decided to drag my feet for a hundred miles.

Part III
End of the Pilgrim
1 August 2011
Chapter 1: The Phoenix.

Thoughts of useless lawyers crossed my mind on day three of the Pilgrimage, as I lay in the grass, defeated. My calves and mind strained past the testing limit. I passed pain yesterday; I left him behind on the roadside, told him I had had enough, I set myself free from his company and kept walking.

Pain was not so easily shaken though. He caught back up with me the following day. I thought my problem was physical and not mental, but never trust the mind when it says, "give up." I had 10,000 excuses to give up on this walk and only one or two reasons to finish. Limits are mostly mental. Those bleeding feet and contracted muscles were real, but my mental power was greater. Greater than a few blisters. Nothing to brag about, but yet rising from the ground took all the strength I had.

Survival stories have always grabbed my attention. I have read a few books on the subject: Shackleton, Krakauer, Ralston, Simpson and Callaghan. There are common themes that exist among survivors.

One such theme is making small achievable goals. Self-esteem thrives on the success of achieved goals. I use this same philosophy in education. People want to feel success. As a teacher, I guided my students towards success, as a father, I did the same.

A comprehensive look at the subject of survival can be found in the book, <u>Deep Survival: Who Lives, Who Dies and Why</u>, by Laurence Gonzales.

Simpson crawled for three days over glacier rock with his femur staring at him; Shackleton planned his North Pole Expedition while watching his ship, *Endurance*, splinter and sink below the ice near the South Pole. People have achieved amazing feats based on their will to live.

All I had to do was walk a few miles with blisters. I assessed my situation, opened my eyes and saw the help I needed. A little push from the outside pulled a lever in my mind and picked my body up off the ground.

I saw a young pilgrim striding down the highway. He was the first pilgrim I saw on my journey and it was day three. He was in running shorts, a clean t-shirt and flash running shoes. He walked fast and confident, carrying a small backpack like a university student. I rose and caught him. I followed and forgot about the pain.

I was being drawn-in to the power of the movement. I gained strength from the young man and his will.

I started my mantra: "Stretch and stretch and stretch those legs." I lengthened my stride to stretch out my calf muscles. We moved at a good clip and exchanged few words.

I had been a lone pilgrim the past two days. Now I was one among two, benefitting from the strength of the lead dog.

He veered off to do on an errand before he continued on to San Jose. At 10am, I had at least six more hours before I would get to San Jose.

I was reborn through his example.

I never learned his name. I missed him just the same.

Chapter 2: Not a Jealous Wife.

The airport highway is 15 miles long and dead straight. You see blacktop, six lanes wide, until white dotted lines unite and close in on themselves, then touch the horizon; that is where I am going. Color blurred with light on passing cars and trucks, a hazy monoxide mist shrouds my future.

"Hail Mary, Full of grace the Lord is with thee. Jesus Christ please help my son Sean."

My last gas station stop, I bought water, peanut M & M's and a couple of bananas. I recalled this road as having miles of auto lots selling used cars from the USA: Toyotas, Cherokees and Troopers aside all makes of Hyundai's. With the 6 mile stretch of auto lots come the garages that work body and engine. I passed battalions of auto yard dogs that barked on ceremony.

I reckoned there had food stands or convenience stores along the way for the black booted mechanics, but not so, there was not one restaurant or shop on that stretch and the noon sun was cooking with gas.

I was lucky to meet a fiftyish looking Tico riding a mountain bike wearing high speed riding gear. He was not out for riding hard, he was soft and pleasant. He had the means to look the part and tell his buddies or wife that he was out, "riding."

He reminded me of one of Soledad's cousins. He was married with grown children, salt of the earth, educated Tico who worked hard for a big company and enjoyed an upper middle class lifestyle.

He was known as a devoted mountain biker although he never looked like a hard-core anything to me. He was middle management soft. The truth came to light that the bulk of his biking for twelve years was round-trip every weekend to his girlfriend's house. He lived a long lie to his wife. Persistent deception is enormous cargo and deceiving a trusting spouse for over a decade must weigh heavy on the conscience.

There is no dignity, no heart, no love nor self-respect in lying and cheating. Nothing is worthy of tarnishing your soul. There are shades of grey where the moral compass may swing off-center of north but cheating on your wife for 12 years ain't got no wiggle room in anyone's Fair Play Handbook. Cheating and lying is lowland bog trekking, keep your soul shoes clean and stick to the moors of moral high ground and at the same time, and most importantly, learn to reserve judgment. Judge no man. The foibles and failures of others are their business only, not pretty feathers to be put in your cap for vanity's sake, nor arrows in your quiver for future attacks disguised as defense.

His wife was known as a jealous woman. After his hidden betrayal was revealed, she didn't really seem that jealous at all.

I had heard about fellows like this, from cultures like France and Brazil. I suppose Latin American culture in general has a high probability of infidelity.

My beacon will always be the light of my conscience. Not everyone sees your light and that can be a problem too.

I am vilified in my wife's eyes. The lowest of the low, lower that the scags of Scotland and yet my conscience is clear. I imagine her conscience is perfectly clear as well.

Life can be funny like that: contrasting perspectives on reality. With communication bridging those perspectives, there is hope of a mutually agreeable relationship, without communication those perspectives remain anchored in distance water, far past hope of signal flags or lighthouses with no longboats to deliver messages.

At the time, I wasn't occupied by the possible infidelities of the bike rider nor maritime metaphors. I was interested in water. I asked him if he knew where I could buy something to drink. He looked up the road and down the road, chewed his moustache, squinted his eyes and as sweat dripped off his brow said, "No. No hay." "No, there is none."

He did offer his water and on his encouragement, I killed the bottle.

I thanked him, got his opinion on the distance to San Jose and we parted friends.

He blessed my way and I his.

"Jesus Christ, please help my daughter Elizabeth."

Chapter 3: Walking the White Line.

I arrived at the outskirts of La Uruca, where Abuelo lives right down the street from my mother-in-law's house, where my wife and children live. The Restraining Order had not yet been delivered, so I was free to go to my mother-in-law's house and knock on the door and hope to see the children.

I didn't do that because of what they may witness in the process: My wife's anger, my tears and if I tried to stay, the arrival of the police, then me with cuffed hands trying to wave goodbye and the children left with the imagine of the back of my head in a police car.

The other reason I didn't try to break-in to my children's lives is because children need a vision of the future. To arrive one day and then not re-appear for two weeks and then reappear and disappear without consistency would be traumatic for my children, more traumatic than not seeing me at all, at least that was my reasoning at the time.

The courts would grant me visits soon enough, so why cloud the water?

This court process bled me slowly with false hope.

I sought out measures to provide consistency and a plan for the well-being of my children. We communicated about the past and present and the future during our family meetings.

Family Meetings

"Uncle" Billy comes from an educated family. His father is a doctor of education and his mother has about 83 university degrees. Uncle Billy told me his parents held family meetings when he was growing up and now that he is a father, he does the same. I employ the customs of happy families into my own life, because "all happy families are alike," and I wanted my family to be one among them.

Over time, we failed as a happy family and were "unhappy in our own way" (Anna Karenina, Tolstoy).

Our first family meeting started in our living room on a Saturday morning. The boys were still in pajamas. We sat down and I started, "Ok, the first Murphy Family meeting is underway. Everybody gets a chance to talk. When somebody else is talking please pay attention. One person speaks at a time."

Ted jumps in.

"Papá, can I eat a cookie?"

Teddy is the food guy. He is the one for whom I leave bananas on the table. He is the reason we stored cookies and chocolate low in the cupboards for ease of access. He loves fruit and I love that about him.

He makes me smile and he makes me proud.

"Ok, there is a motion on the floor. Ted would like refreshments served during the meetings. Mamá, what do you think? Should we serve refreshments during the meetings?"

The boys waited with eyes wide in hopeful expectation for the word from our queen. We also called Soledad, "The Boss." There was no doubt about who made decisions in our kingdom. We all deferred to my wife.

Soledad said, "I vote, 'Yes,' for food."

Ted went to get cookies and he passed them out with momentary satisfaction.

"Papá, what about a juice box?" Sean asked.

"Motion on the floor for beverages."

Hands shoot up and Sean gets juice boxes from the kitchen.

The first five minutes of our first family meeting and my boys both felt empowered. This is a custom a happy family nurtures.

Our first family decision had been made: "Ok, food and drink will be served at the meetings." We had accomplished effective communication.

Everyone spoke and everyone was listened to. We mapped out our lives and the coming weeks ahead with birthdays and holidays and visits to family.

Meetings maintain communication and provide the forum to address individual and familial goals and objectives. What are we working on personally?

Sean is hitting Ted, Ted is not eating dinner, both are dragging bottoms in the morning, it is too dangerous for Sean to wake up in the darkness and stumble half asleep down the stairs to sleep with Papá in the basement, (he did this every night for months). These were our issues that we worked to improve. Improvement was noted and appreciated and new goals were set and as new challenges presented themselves, we continued to refine our personal development as a Community (Family) of Learners.

Family Meetings were impromptu and any member of the family could call for a family meeting.

After Elizabeth was born, Soledad stopped participating in Family Meetings. We had lost our Queen. It was a downfall for us all that one of our members no longer bought-in. We still held the meetings. We still addressed needs and goals but a piece of the communication started to die. When communication dies the relationship is soon to follow.

Chapter 4: Visiting Abuelo.

I wanted Abuelo to know what I was doing and what I was willing to do. I was still seeking approval in my life and I wanted his.

I was fearful of seeing Soledad or the children. I would wear this fear for the next year and a half of my life. Fear of being arrested at any minute.

The fear only grew worse after the restraining order was in effect. Any time I went into San Jose, I was fearful of running into my children and wife. She could call the police and file a report that I was stalking, subsequently lengthening the one year Restraining Order.

Just a bit of bad timing could sequester my children from me for an additional six months.

But since the Restraining Order had not yet been delivered, I knocked on Abuelo's door and he answered and gave me a hug and a kiss.

He was having lunch with Abuela and Tio Antonio. They were seated at the table and I greeted everyone and I asked for a glass of water. I was wearing dirty shorts, a soiled and sweaty long sleeve white button down and carried a battered rucksack tied together with radio wire I found on the side of the road (the zipper broke in route…any port in a storm). I looked like a guy who had walked about 60 miles in three days.

After drinking four glasses of tap water and explaining that I was on the Romeria from Jaco, I kissed Abuelo and Abuela and took my leave.

No one asked me to stay for lunch.

"Hail Mary, full of grace, the Lord is with thee…"

Chapter 5: Doña Ana.

Walking away was more than just emotionally painful. It is almost a mile to get out of Abuelo's neighborhood and two miles round-trip is a long way after 60. I feared my wife would pass in the car, I had a vision of the boys looking out the window as they passed: "It's Papá! It's Papá!"

Those "what if's" are what haunts the mind, the possibilities prompting tears. I refocused my efforts and started to pray to bring myself into the present.

I read that depression is a result of living in the past and anxiety a product of worrying about the future. It has been years and I am still trying to keep my mind in the present. It is a daily exercise.

"The Lord is with thee…"

My next stop would be the used electronics/hardware shop of my friend Steven. He is "Tio Steve" to my family. He is a half gringo, half Tico (Costa Rican). His father is a gringo doctor and his mother comes from hard working merchant stock. His grandmother owns a hardware chain in Costa Rica.

Steve and I visited with his grandmother, Doña Ana, three weeks before, when I first arrived in Costa Rica. She is 80 but looks 60 and is still sharp as a splinter. She has the values of Warren Buffet and lives in the same humble home that she lived in before she was wealthy.

We sat at her kitchen table and she brought out food and coffee. Steve briefed her on my tale and then she told me hers.

She and her husband opened one hardware store together. They had five children and built the store up until her husband ran off with the secretary. She was a single mother in the 1950's in Costa Rica. She was also a business owner.

She dealt with the shame of having her husband run-off by making a successful business and then a lucrative business and then a mini-empire. She lived the mother's side of explaining to the children that Papá was no longer a part off their lives. From what I gathered, he just forgot about the children, but I find that hard to believe.

She lived through a challenging experience and came out shining like a new penny.

She said she cried for over a year and every day she went to work and tried to forget the past and look towards the future. She took small steps everyday (just like the survival manuals say to do). If you are alone in the rain forest or going through divorce in the 50's, the method for survival is the same: set small achievable goals. Doña Ana didn't let the foolish tragedy of her past affect how she was going to live her life in the future. We all get dealt a shite hand now and again. Everyone, without fail, has tragedy in their lives. There is no life without pain and Doña Ana took her lumps.

She built the business by steady progress and hard work. There was a need and she filled it and now has the luxury of time and money to sit with her grandson and his broken friend on a Tuesday morning.

She hugged me and gave me advice. "This will all end soon. Where do you want to be when your children are ready to see you again? Get to that place. God Bless."

Doña Ana and Wayne Gretzky have the same formula for success. Wayne Gretzky is one of the greatest goal scorers in Professional Hockey History. When asked what made him great he said, "I am never where the puck is, I am always where the puck is going to be."

I am not now where my children are, but I am where they will be and I am ready for their arrival.

Chapter 6: Steve's Shop.

I arrived at Steve's shop in downtown San Jose on a defunct side street that used to bustle but now houses two last hold-out stores: one of them is Steve's and the other belongs to his mother. All the stores and lots have been bought up to build a high-rise, but since Steve is grandfathered in and never had a lease to begin with, it is tough to get him out.

The shop is a social place where penniless Ticos and ex-pats drink coffee and wine with rich gringos, hard Germans, French recluses, fighter pilots and artists.

I arrived to a big hug and questions about my appearance. I was muted from the concentration of three days walking. I sat in the King's chair and fielded questions:

Them: "What the hell happened to you?"
Me: "I have been walking for three days from Jaco."
Them: "Jaco! Are you totally nuts? You walked from Jaco and didn't get killed?

The conversation moved like this with rapid fire questions for a while. I felt pilgrim light envelope me. I was beyond where I was sitting and the questions. I was in a zone of profound peace and quiet. I spoke slowly.

Present that day was a seasoned veteran Tico father in his 50's. I haven't seen him since. He was a working class Tico, a bachelor in dress slacks with dusty shoes and children he didn't know.

He was reserved in his advice but gave it anyway. He said, "Give up on the court system and forget about your children. Forget about them, it is the best you can do. If she wants them, forget about them."

He gave some details of his life, he too had lived the wife wanting the children and he just walked away. It is the frequency of Ticos (men) walking away that has moved the Ticas (women) to believe that children don't need a father.

It is true. Children do not need a father. Children don't "need" much to survive. (See Maslow's Hierarchy of Needs.) Children don't need to learn to read, children don't need to eat more than 1200 calories a day, children don't need to play sports or ride bikes, children don't need to know their father or their mother and for that matter, there are plenty of children surviving in orphanages.

Proving what children "Need" and "Don't Need," is easy.

Providing what is optimal is the goal. Can we provide the optimal for our children?

Being satisfied with basic needs is setting the bar pretty low for someone with first world access to education and opportunities. Moving forward into higher order Maslow Needs so as to produce an individual prepared for emotional, physical and intellectual success is where we want to dance together as parents. This mantra of "Children Don't Need a Father," that I had been hearing from all walks of Tico life is base. I was ignorant to the concept. A large swath of Costa Rica has been functioning under the premise that, "Children don't need a father," for generations. I just didn't know it. I arrived late to the party, wearing white after Labor Day.

At the time I was not willing to take the seasoned veteran's advice, I couldn't "Forget about my children." Another full year and five months would pass before I finally took half of his advice.

I fought the good fight for a year and a half with the Court System until I realized the game was rigged and stepped away from the table. I could have lived in Costa Rica perpetually treading water, waiting to see the children, I was prepared for the extreme marathon of Costa Rican Justice; only after I was faced with prison, did I decide to withdraw from the game.

For the moment though, as a pilgrim with a mere two months in country, I was still filled with hope and potential.

Hope and potential manifested themselves during this pilgrimage. I felt empowered by my expression of will. I had invested in the flesh and blood of action.

There was but one more day to walk. It was Monday and the Feast of the Negrita was the next day. I had arrived.

The walk from San Jose to the Basilica in Cartago was about a six hour march. I had walked 12, 15 and 10 hours the last three days. I felt like I could hold my breath and walk for 6 hours.

I went to the Hemingway Hotel in downtown San Jose. It is a small inexpensive affair, housed in an old mansion with small rooms chopped up from a three story Spanish Colonial layout. I liked the name.

I spoke with the owner and an Englishman in the lobby, explaining that I had walked from Jaco. The Englishman told me about his six week walk on El Camino de Santíago, a pilgrimage in Spain. I had walked for three days and had already had enough.

I took my key, thanked the owner and the Englishman and put El Camino de Santíago on my list of things I would never do. This walk was a one shot deal. I would be with my children within a year. At the time I didn't even consider the possibility that the courts could keep me from my children for a full year more.

I write this now, in Mexico, and am paralyzed at the thought of the person I was then, with hopes and expectations that I would be reunited with my children. I was a teacher, a principal and most importantly, a father invested in being present in the everyday lives of his children. How could I not be reunited with my children?

My relationship with my wife aside, (as it should be), I was a good father.

I was ignorant and idealistic (both springboards to disappointment) standing in the lobby of The Hemingway, three days worn of road dirt and pain, expecting that I would see my children in the next three weeks. It couldn't take longer than that for some type of communication to be effectuated for the sake of humanity. Right?

There had to be a provision for supervised visits and phone calls. There were and I was waiting with hope. Could be three days, three weeks or three months and that is the anxiety I lived with. Now, three years seems more likely. I haven't given up hope but I now have realistic expectations. I expect little from life and even less from my wife and nothing from the Costa Rican Justice System.

If a future seeing pixie had told me that the following year I would still be without my children, with no clear expectation of seeing them, I would have started a hunger strike, I would have sat in front of the courthouse until I was permitted to communicate with my children.

There was no crystal ball, no pixie dust or potion and there is no champagne smoking lounge for the financially able: I was in the shite, ignorant, but far from blissful. I had one more day to walk to the Virgin. Maybe she can help me.

"Hail Mary, full of grace, the Lord is with thee…"

Chapter 7: Family Tree.

Eyes open. Pain. Pray.

Clear skies and a bright sun. Where were Sean and Ted and Elizabeth? Were they waking-up now? Having breakfast? What would they do today? I was their father but I didn't know. I couldn't know. I couldn't go near them, call them, or look at them from afar.

What were they told and what did they think and know? What was their vision for our future?

The last words Sean spoke to me rent the curtains of my soul: "Papá, where are you?"

I cried. I dressed. I prayed.

I answered aloud to no one at all: I am walking this pilgrimage today Sean. I am proving my will.

I checked out by 6:30am and bought my breakfast at the AM/PM Mini-Mart (the 7-11 of Costa Rica). I bought peanuts and bananas and yogurt and Gatorade and a roll with butter and peanut M&M's. I was ready for the day as I sat on a bench two blocks from the courthouse. I would intimately know that courthouse in the coming year and four months until I decided that any hope of justice coming from that building was impossible. I gave the court system one year and six months of my life hoping that lady justice would serve my children, that their rights to know their father would be upheld.

After a year and a half of waiting and hoping to see my children I would take drastic measures but at the time, sitting on the bench, on the last day of my pilgrimage, I watched the families walk past. Good Christians walking together. Some families were three generations with grandmothers in tow.

What did my children know and remember of my family? What do they know of me? How could they know, how can I tell them? The stories about my family were born that morning, so my children will have an idea from whence they came, our family tree, their family name.

I remembered my grandmother, Margaret Dougherty and her three children: my mother and my two long dead uncles. I remember them like this:

Blowing My Family Nose Tree

Like all activities with my children, time and interest are the two most important factors. If I was interested, they were interested.

I have a runny nose. It runs in the summer, spring, winter and in the fall I am still trying to catch this nose. I always have some nose wipe on hand: hanky, sleeve, tissue or t-shirt. I started carrying hankies when I was about 36 years old.

I carried one for show and one for blow. The secret pride of preparedness appeals to my Boy Scout nature. The hanky is Jesus, a savior, a life raft in a storm of runny snot and hanging boogies. Having something relevant to pull out of your pocket in an awkward social emergency is important.

Some people carry tissues. Gram Doc, my grandmother, was a spindly 80 year old tissue carrier with white hair when I knew her. She died when I was 9 or 10, so my memories of her are born young and ended early. She wore cardigan sweaters in pale blue or white. From years of use the yarn had stretched comfortable and long, to fall past her waist. The sleeves too, had grown long, but those were easily rolled to meet her thin, blue veined wrists. She kept tissues tucked into her sleeves. Margaret Dougherty bore three children: Edward, James and Joan. Joan is my mother. Her brothers were like this:

Uncle Ed was first a Park Guard and then a City Cop in Philadelphia. He was a big, likeable, stereotypical Irish Cop. He had a red nose and a good sized belly and clear blue eyes that smiled.

I never saw Uncle Ed without a beer. For visits outside his home, he carried an auxiliary case of beer on ice, in the trunk of his car, because only commercial establishments (bars, taverns or tap rooms) could stock the quantity of beer necessary to quench his thirst.

I now know he was a "working alcoholic" as opposed to messy drunks who can't hold down a job because the drink has got em'. I don't know how he handled work. I doubt that he drank at work although it wouldn't be out of the question for old school coppers to stop and have a drink for lunch or a Park Guard to have a nip of whiskey to warm the belly on cold winter nights while sitting alone in the small guardhouse shack with the potbellied stove.

When I was nine, I marveled over how much he liked beer. I felt that way too, about Hubba Bubba bubble gum and Whoppers. Teddy likes his bananas and Sean Chinese Chicken (General Chows Chicken). I marveled at Uncle Ed's unnatural thirst. I didn't know about alcoholism at the time, but I knew something was wrong. No man should be that thirsty.

His brother, my children's Great Uncle Jimmy, on the other hand (or maybe on the same alcoholic hand; just a different finger) was a hard liquor alcoholic. This guy was a likeable, happy drunk, unless he was in a fight with someone, then he was not so likeable. He was short and cocky from the rodeo pics that I have seen of him. He died when I was in first grade. My father, Pop, was at a horse show and here is how he tells of meeting Uncle Jim and how Uncle Jim had a sister who Pop would later meet and love and marry: Joan Murphy, my mother.

Here is Pop's story, which is one possible starting point for all of our stories:

I was at a horse show at Marlin Frances on Welsh Rd. I seen 3 big dudes laying on a blanket and another one standing lookin' down at this little guy.

People were gathering around and the little guy was saying, "Come back in the woods. I don't want to fight you with your friends here."

It was in the afternoon. I was on my horse. I edged closer and said, "Go ahead, n' belt him Shorty! Nobody will bother you."

I guess they sensed if they tried, they'd get stomped as later people found out that I could run that horse into a wall if I wanted. I mean nothin' could stop her if I wanted her to do you.

Jim got punched in his big beak and it was all over. I rode away. Jim got his horse, came riding up to me and said, "My name is Jim Dougherty. What yours?"

"Joe Murphy," I said, "You didn't fair to well. Why'd you punch him?"

He said, "I looked up at you and that horse and said to myself, "There's one with me!"

That started a lifetime friendship.

These are 1940's cowboys living in Philadelphia. There was a "horse people" community living within the city limits. The parks connected everything straight through to the state capital of Harrisburg, PA. The distance is about 100 hard walking miles, much like my current pilgrimage. You could travel on horse trails for a week.

And with that, my father connected to his future wife and after four children and two decades, I was born and 32 years later Sean was begat. Such is the family tree, which starts in this tale with Gram Doc and her tissues.

Joe Murphy bronc riding circa 1948.

My Gram Doc had clear blue eyes with hazel around the edges. I remember her eyes being as watery as her nose, but I am sure she dazzled in her youth, before her eyes and nose went leaky from wear and forced her to surreptitiously tuck tissues in the sleeve of her worn woven cardigans.

You have to teach young people to blow their noses. The first nose blowing practice with Sean and Ted didn't involve any tissues. The lesson started in the bathtub. The three of us would strip down and fill-up the tub. All my life, I had never taken a bath with more than two inches of water. Since I came from a family of five, I guess that was necessary, but my boys liked a good 6 inches or more. We bathed in deep water and I loved it.

We put our faces under water and blew bubbles from our nose or took big open mouth inhales and then slowly submerged past the nose but under the eyes. Sometimes we sat so still the water line remained constant to submerge our mouth but leave our nose breathing, carefully balancing life between two atmospheres.

We looked into each other's eyes and focused on our not breathing. They learned to breathe out of their noses, how to hold their breath, and to become familiar with the burn of lungs wanting oxygen. Learning the anatomy of breathing was the first step in nose blowing.

We took turns to challenge how long we could stay underwater with our full face submerged. It was another step in being comfortable in water. This was not only bath time and nose blowing practice; this was also the first swimming lesson. Swimming is first about managing breath and secondly about moving body parts. Young children have the strength to swim; the problem is they do not understand how to manage their breathing and then they panic and then they sink.

The boys formed the habit of inhaling through their mouth and exhaling through their nose; which also clears the nasal passages like blowing your nose without a tissue. The boys were blowing their noses from instinct to clear out the airways that they now knew they possessed.

We practiced breathing five nights a week in the tub. We spent that time together and learned to breathe and the only other part of the nose blowing lesson is how to hold a tissue. That took about nothing to learn. We then honed in on the finer points of nose blowing like nostril rotation for maximum output. We still checked each other's noses for the stray boogie but the boys were both grabbing their own tissues and blowing away. Mamá was proud of her boys.

We learned the anatomy of the breathe, the art of breathing and how to blow a nose in the tub, at night, after dinner, noiselessly sitting ever so still with the warm soapy water up to our eyeballs, when all was right with our world.

Chapter 8: No Helmets.

The streets teamed with pilgrims like all the little ants marching towards their goal. I was one among hundreds, thousands. There were young couples clutching water bottles, teenagers running and laughing. Old and young mothers pushed strollers, while fathers in white tennis shoes wearing white socks and jean shorts lathered sunscreen on resistant toddlers.

There was an innocuous gang of 7-10 kids on bicycles, older brothers on trick bikes and younger siblings hanging on to the fringe of the crowd. I took in the breath of Costa Ricans, all walking towards the Virgin.

The kids were laughing and yelling and riding wheelies for as long as they could. I thought about of one of the complaints against me in the family court. I had allowed my sons to ride their bicycles without helmets. Just once.

At the beach in Jaco, Costa Rica, everyone rides bicycles. Mothers peddle while four year olds stand on the center rails of beach cruisers. I saw a baby in a front basket which made me gasp. I have a friend who rides his two children to school every day with his 7 year old son standing on the pegs connected to the back wheel and his four year old daughter sitting side saddle on the center rail like a good little lady.

I saw a family of four on a motorcycle with the mother balancing a propane tank in her lap. What I didn't see on any of these folk were helmets.

My children were taken away and one of the points worthy of citing to the judges was that I once let the children ride without helmets. I felt the meaning of Kafkaesque. My life was a Dada painting theme with no dots connecting the events to reality. I marched on, praying and thinking of my children. Were they riding bikes this morning? Who would fix their bike if it broke? Who would teach Elizabeth to ride? Who would teach Ted when he was ready to take off the training wheels?

My wife never learned to ride a bike. I felt the injustice and I felt the emotional pain and I walked on, alone with my suffering, one among a larger crowd of many suffering.

We all have our stories. There is no life without pain.

"...of grace, the Lord is with thee..."

Chapter 9: The Virgin Speaks.

We were all walking for a reason. You don't walk 6 hours without one. In Spanish, the word is, "Prometa." If you walk and finish the pilgrimage you get to ask a favor. I don't know the Virgin's success rate but she sure takes her time. If the Virgin didn't come up big for you then the Prometa certainly wasn't in your best interest. Or you can just keep waiting, like I am.

The Virgin may help you out with your miracle: cancer cures and alcoholism, bad bunions and bad boys, lost souls and job seekers. You can ask the virgin for anything. But will she give? How long will her giving take? If one is not spiritually prepared to receive the gift, time can become an enemy.

I have been three years in the waiting, but when I am reunited with my children, I will quietly thank the Virgin for whatever hand she has taken in my miracle among the millions at her little black feet.

I was stride for stride with a young man. He was a university student and had been on the walk before. We were climbing uphill to Cartago. The last 3 kilometers to Cartago are all uphill. The effort at the end is fitting for the trial of the past three days.

We approached the basilica and it was elbow to elbow with pilgrims. People from all socio economic levels and ages had come to the festival area of the Romeria. The front of the church was like a crowded country fair.

I separated from my new friend and found the line to enter the church. I was on the verge of completing my journey and I felt the fullness of the realization and the quietness of the Pilgrim and in a few minutes I would be face to rock with the little statue.

From the entrance of the church until the display of the Virgin at the nave, all pilgrims walk on their knees. Everyone else was doing it. I went with the flow.

It was painful. My walking-friend warned me that the last 50 yards on your knees is a bitch. I was in so much pain from the previous days; ten minutes of kneeling couldn't touch me. I thought.

The tiles offer no comfort or congratulations, still, I had done finished.

But what had a gained? What was the message?

I was praying and kneeling along with the others in a slow procession.

"Hail Mary, full of grace, the Lord is with thee…"

The Basilica is a domed affair. The light was gold. There are small windows circling the main dome and the side dome and the walls up high. There must be a hundred little windows. The inner domes are gold leafed so the light is born golden and doesn't have a choice. The light assaulted me from all angles. I drifted up to the windows on a bed of gold and came back down to approach the little black rock.

The Basilica of Our Lady of the Angels.

My mind was clear, my heart was opened and the Virgin spoke to me. My epiphany came in a profound wave.

"Life is Pain. Get used to it."

Life is pain. Get used to it.

The statue was a dud. I don't even think I really got a good look at her. What I do remember was the light.

I crossed myself, stood and walked away. I took my message and a bus home.

I had completed the walk. The Virgin had spoken.

I went on that walk to express what I was willing to do to be a father present in the everyday lives of his children.

I had engaged in the court process hoping for salvation. The judges would save me from pain, my wife would come around and save me, my wife's family would save me, my patience would save me, justice would save me, the virgin would save me.

No one would save me.

Life is pain, get used to it.

I would get used to the pain of injustice, the pain of the abduction of my children, the pain of not knowing where they are and with whom they are learning and living, the pain of the loss of my identity, the pain of lost time. Time can never be recovered or repaid. Lost time is an absolute.

I could only save myself.

The pain will not go away, it has diminished with time as I write this three years out, but that year and three months in Costa Rica after my pilgrimage, after the Virgin had spoken, beat me down, chopped me up, stripped me naked with hands tied behind, that year of waiting and hoping for justice and fighting the good fight while never seeing or speaking with my children…seeking salvation…it was all just an exercise in my epiphany.

I would get used to the pain. There was no other way. The Virgin's message to me was pure truth.

"Hail Mary, full of grace, the Lord is with thee…Please help my son Sean and my son Ted and my daughter Elizabeth."

Part IV

Costa Rican Justice

September 7, 2011

Chapter 1: Domestic Violence?

What I have learned and what I have lost? My concept of Domestic Violence was the drunken husband coming home and smacking the old lady around, like De Niro in "Raging Bull" or Brando in, "On the Waterfront."

I considered Domestic Violence as closed fist, slap or backhand, a good shove, but definitely skin on skin or at least the threat to do harm. I believed Domestic Violence needed *some threat of physical harm*. I thought threatening words to intimidate like, "I am gonna knock yer fucking head off...," or, "If you ever leave, I'll kill you...myself...your mom." Not so, and not even close.

I have seen, "Sleeping with the Enemy," and recognize that Psychological Abuse exists, but I wasn't checking the alphabetical order of the cans in the cupboards or limiting my wife's ability to live her life as she saw fit.

In Costa Rica, Domestic Violence requires three words from the wife: I was afraid.

Done deal. Don't pass go, don't collect your $200 cause' you are cut off from your children and your home.

I just arrived home from school in Costa Rica and my friend called me to say that the police were looking for me at Pizza Palma, the shop owned by my two dearest friends in Jaco Beach. "No problem," I said, "I'll be right over." I only lived two blocks from the place so I arrived quickly.

Three police officers were on site, two big guys with hard faces and a young lady cop. They took one look at the gringo they assume beats his wife and nobody was smiling. The big guys looked eager and edged into my personal space. Lady cop was accompanied by my wife's friend, Elena Susia, who is a lawyer. They asked for my name and my identification and served me with a Restraining Order.

Restraining Order? The papers were from the Domestic Violence Court of San Jose. Domestic Violence: I have one tattoo and it is a peace symbol. I have never in my life laid hands on a woman. I have never threatened a woman physically or emotionally in my life –not even close.

The lawyer who served me with the papers, my wife's friend, came to my house to visit and stayed with us for 10 days just two years before. I cooked for her; I drove her to see sights and cleaned her dishes. She saw me with my sons. She saw me reading to them, bathing them, feeding and playing with my children; she saw the connection and love that we had for each other. She lived with us for 10 days or so and never, at any point did she say to my wife, "You should get the hell out of here because this guy is dangerous."

From my conversations with Elena during her stay with us, I sensed her jealousy towards my wife. My wife had two houses and two beautiful children and husband who bathed and fed and put the kids to bed. I didn't drink or spend any time away from my children that was not related to my job as a teacher. Elena was overweight, single, bitter and didn't wash her face quite enough.

I said to Elena, "You stayed with us, you lived with us for two weeks. Did you ever see signs of Domestic Violence?"

She said, "Everything you have done since is Domestic Violence John."

"Great," I thought, "another person who forgets what they saw but is willing to believe the contrary."

I asked her again, "Did you ever see signs of Domestic Violence when you were with us?" It didn't matter. I signed the docs and they went away.

Chapter 2: Third Lawyer.

I had struck out badly with my first two lawyers. I was telling my tale to my friend's girlfriend, Sophia. She is a dentist who comes from a family of teachers. She is good Costa Rican stock, so I figured she had an inroad.

Sophia said Betty Verga was an excellent lawyer who is super communicative and uses texts and email and has been on top of Sophia's case for two years. Great, give me her number.

I met with Ms. Verga at a local mall food court. She works in a lawyer's office but this case she would take on the side, so the food court doubled as her office.

My first impression was that she looked to come from upper middle class means. She was tallish and well-groomed and well dressed. She looked a lot like my friend's girlfriend and was just as vain. We sat down together as I took her in. My God, she was wearing colored contacts.

My new lawyer wants to be model and changes her eye color. This could get messy.

I didn't have another option present and Sophia said she was good, so the hell with it. I was pushing the ball up the hills in the courts. I needed someone to file the papers.

I told her my tale. She sat and judged me and took notes. I didn't recognize the judgment for what it was, I never got used to her condemning judgment. I now see that as a big problem in the lawyer client relationship.

We exchanged hundreds of emails. She was very communicative and responsive and I liked that. She just lacked experience and intelligence. Three memories stand out.

She wore big red hoop earrings to the Domestic Violence hearing and her lime green silk panties made an appearance during the hearing. Great, my lawyer has her panties hanging out.

Second, during the 6 supervised visits with my children, Ted said this, "Papá, I went to sleep the night before my birthday and I wished that you would come. And you didn't."

Those were the saddest words I had heard in my life.

During the visit, after Ted said that, Sean said, "It is because Papá doesn't know where we live."

I love Sean. He tried to come to my rescue. He tried to help me but I wasn't focused at the time. I was frustrated that anyone would subject Ted to such a level of disappointment and I was taking the blame.

I said to Sean, in a flat tone, "I know where you live Sean." And I put my face in my hands and cried. How did I arrive to have my children taken from me? Others were making decisions and their decisions were causing my child pain.

In the transcripts of the visits there is but one negative mark for me and that was my response to Sean.

I met with my lawyer and we went over the transcripts. She wanted to know why I reacted that way. I started crying and couldn't stop. I could only point to the words before what I said, the highlighted words of my son Ted. To date, the saddest words I have ever heard: "I wished you would come..."

I sat with my lawyer and cried and she said, "If you can't talk, I can't help." She was angry. I pointed again to what Ted said and she said, "Yeah, that's what he said. Why did you react to Sean?"

She was so cold, with no empathy. I was traumatized and paralyzed by sorrow.

I told her the meeting was over and I left. "Go then," she said.

She became worthless to me.

My lawyer was a heartless ex model who can't keep her panties in check during a Domestic Violence Hearing. She is on the fast track to becoming a judge in Costa Rica. There is little doubt that she could adequately fill the position. It is no wonder this thing wasn't working out for me. I didn't have the money to make any other moves and I am certain that a lawyer wasn't going to make much difference in the system.

"Pray for us sinners. Now and at the hour of our death."

Chapter 3: The Magic Words: I was afraid.

There are usually three separate courts involved in any divorce in Costa Rica: Family, Domestic Violence and Child Support. The garbage truck of Family Court deals with visitation and includes Social Services and Psychologists who stand on the back, tossing in reports.

The second court is Domestic Violence Court. If you want to get a divorce in Costa Rica you will most likely find yourself attacking or defending in Domestic Violence Court because lawyers use the proceeding to gain higher ground. For those of Soledad's culture, Domestic Violence is an automatic.

Lawyer says to female potential clients, "Do you want him out of your house (it is hers now) and away from the kids?"

"It's before noon. I can have him restricted from the house by the time he gets home from work."

It is a piece of cake and common knowledge for Costa Ricans. I wasn't Costa Rican and didn't know enough of the culture.

Forget any yardstick and use this as the litmus test: All the wife has to say is: I was afraid.

"I was afraid," will seal the Domestic Violence case. Judges have no interest in risking that a man could react badly. If the woman says she is afraid then the judge acts accordingly. Good nuff'.

I get it.

My wife was never in any danger from me and anyway, if I was bat shit crazy to kill her, a piece of paper wasn't going to be a deal breaker.

Requesting a Domestic Violence Restraining Order as Auxiliary proceeding to an initial Divorce Filing sucks resources away from women who actually have black eyes for not having the beans ready. In the take-a-number line at the Domestic Violence Office, women who have taken a punch in the nose are waiting in line behind me and my wife's lawyer for face time with an overworked clerk.

I sat among the abused women in Domestic Violence office and thought of the travesty of abusing the system and gumming up the works for real victims. U.S. Federal maxim: Frivolous fear is not a lawful excuse.

Truth be told, the only person who hit anyone in our marriage was my wife hitting me. It happened once, early on. Truth and justice as they pertain to the legal system are but fodder for philosophers and first year law students and have little to do with legal system outcomes.

Financial abuse is also considered a form of control. My wife had a bank card and a minivan and her mother lived 20 minutes away. So cross off the financial abuse as well. I did not restrict my wife's movements or life by any degree of the law.

I told her, "There is the door. If you want to leave you can use it." That statement counts for upholding a restraining order and my wife wins.

What does she win?

She wins the right to cut me off from speaking or seeing my children for one year. I cannot visit, call, visit the schools, contact her family, send emails or question about the health of Sean, a childhood cancer survivor. Nothing.

Out for one year.

It came to pass on a morning in the Domestic Violence office in the courthouse in San Jose. Any man who walks into that office loses.

I saw my wife in the hallway before the hearing. She walked past and I said, "Hello." She looked like she still was not getting nearly enough sleep. She was a mess and I felt terrible to see her like that. I felt sick that she was experiencing pain. The shell of a person who just passed me was my wife. I knew that she was not well. The one person who knew her and was willing to do anything for her was me.

And by law, I couldn't even speak with her.

My lawyer was called in to speak with the judge before I was admitted. My wife was requesting that she testify without my presence because she was too afraid to be in the same room with me.

I sat out in the hallway and wondered why I wasn't allowed in there. Am I so scary? Am I so crazy that I would jump the table and go for her throat?

That's what Soledad wanted the judge to believe.

I figured it was her guilty conscience. She just couldn't look me in the eye with all the old bull she was throwing around.

I later learned that this too is Standard Operating Procedure to gain sympathy with the judge. My wife was so traumatized she couldn't be in the same room with me. Wasn't the case over right then? I didn't even need to sit before the judge. Her (the judge's) decision was made.

I went in anyway. I said my peace in Spanish. I had witnesses.

My wife brought her lawyer friend Elena Susia, the one who served me the DV papers, the same woman who stayed with us in Bensalem for two weeks. In regard to the assertion that I drank four times a week:

My Lawyer: How many times did you see Mr. Murphy drink during your stay?

Ms. Susia: Three of us shared a bottle of wine one night.

My Lawyer: So in two weeks you stayed in the house you witnessed Mr. Murphy drink roughly two glasses of wine?

Ms. Susia: That is correct.

At least Elena didn't lie and I am really grateful to her for telling the truth. My wife lied and we just proved she lied by her own witnesses' testimony.

That didn't matter.

I had a letter from the Director of Ted's school saying what a pleasant interview we had and that I paid the tuition on time. The Director refused to say that I did not appear under the influence of drugs. I didn't know at the time that the Psychologist of the school was her daughter. She couldn't openly correct her daughter's letter that said I "smelled of marijuana," although I know she would have liked to. The things we do for our children.

The Director of Sean's school came to the hearing and testified on my behalf.

That didn't matter.

I got the last useless words; I told the judge that I had a clean criminal record in both countries. I was a school teacher and a school principal. I am in the most observed profession that deals with children and my record is without fault.

I said this proceeding is being used as an auxiliary proceeding to the Family Court Visitation Rights that I am requesting. I begged that she consider the rights of my children to know their father.

That didn't matter.

I got the verdict a few days later: Bang went the gavel:

John P. Murphy will not see or speak with Soledad, Sean, Ted or Elizabeth or any of the surrounding family for a period of no less than one year. The date was September 7, 2011.

Bam! Tears for hours.

"Hail Mary, full of grace. The Lord is with you..."

Chapter 4: Family Court.

You get to file three sets of testimony in Family Court. Say whatever you want because you don't need proof to say it. So I file that I want to see the children. Court gives me a Provisional Visitation. My wife rejects and appeals. I then get to say a piece and then she replies and I think is goes one more round until STOP. That back and forth goes on for 4-6 months. It started in July and hit its stride in October. What I would be waiting for as this dialogue takes place is an appointment with the Social Worker (who is a lawyer) and the Psychologist. These folk need to interview all of us and do evaluations and they need to actually write those evaluations.

For the appointment with the Psychologist we were forced to wait for 6 months until March, during which time I could not see or speak with my children.

Six months passes and I have my appointment with the Psych. We laugh, I cry and I expressed my desire to see and speak with my children. It would take her 6 more months to write the report.

Chapter 5: My Dreams and Nightmares.

I felt physical and mental pain from being separated from my children. How was it any different from a kidnapping? Ok, I know they are "safe," but the sense of loss was no less.
I cried daily. I pained daily but I still pushed-on to be ready for the time when my children could see me; the time when my children would have a father, the time when justice would be served.

I did the best I could to improve myself and my career.

The nightmares hurt me to my soul. The emotional pain was an invisible enemy, well-armed and seemingly indestructible.

By prayer, I distracted my mind during the waking hours. You can run from reality but you can't hide from your dreams.

My subconscious created plagues of nightmares for me to process emotionally. One theme was profound loss. The other was feeling like a victim of intense injustice.

The vulnerability of the victim of injustice: How can this happen in a God driven world? Injustice. My dreams confronted injustice, my dreams confronted profound loss. I woke to the reality of loss and injustice and there was no escaping. Life was this nightmare.

If the dark side took a night off and my dreams were of connected, happy times with my children, I awoke to the nightmare of my life.

Either waking up crying or waking up and then crying was the norm.

My dreams were catch-22's from which there was no escape.

Living was a nightmare.

*Right about this time in November, Soledad travels to Montreal to be with Dan Knight. She leaves the kids with someone for 8 days.

Chapter 6: Christmas Visit Torture.

The months between the September 2011 Domestic Violence hearing and the March 2012 appointment with the Psychologist went slowly, painfully, each day another day of unknowing.

Each day I shed another layer of skin, another layer of my connection with my children dissolved. I felt that my identity as a father was slowly dying, but what I learned since is that my need for approval was dying. I was losing faith not in myself or my role as a father but in the system that constrained me and my children.

I never stopped being a father, I stopped seeking approval and when the final layer of approval seeking skin was shed, I was free to act as I saw fit, and that has made all the difference.

Everything with the children was on hold until that March psychologist meeting. My lawyer petitioned that I be permitted to visit with the children in the courthouse to exchange Christmas presents.

The petition was approved by the judge and I lit up quickly but cooled down faster. There was false hope at every turn and I always thought that I would get to see the children but then the rug would get pulled out from under me and I would "tap-out" from the disappointment.

After congratulating me the lawyer said, "We just have to get Soledad notified."

"Oh," I said, "then forget it. It is never going to happen."

The court buildings close on the 12th of December. It was December 3rd when I got the news.

I went shopping for presents for the children. I bought books, and watches that weren't digital, socks and underwear and toothbrushes and cars and balls. I wrapped up all those presents and went to the courthouse to expect my children.

I drove to the courthouse once every couple of weeks for one thing or another. If it wasn't Family Court then it was Domestic Violence or Child Support Court. It is over a two hour drive to get to San Jose from where I lived at the beach in Jaco. It cost over $4 a gallon for diesel fuel, the tolls on the road were over $10 (nothing is cheap in Costa Rica) and parking costs $5-10 a day in the city.

I was used to the ride and I did not want to let my presence be forgotten at the courthouse. By the time I ended my tour with that system, I knew everyone in every office I dealt with. Everyone saw me cry. This isn't just a game of "wait for the papers" to me, every day I was removed from the lives of my children we were victims of a crime.

Time was being stolen from us. The thieves were in plain sight, draped in the garb of justice.

On the Thursday before the Christmas holidays, I showed up at the family court with two bags full of presents.

I sat in the too narrow hallway knowing that I would not see my children. This was a game to all the players. My wife wasn't going to show up by a longshot. So, I looked at my watch and sat and cried. I self-indulged my emotions for a half an hour and wept openly.

The scene was completely pathetic with the presents peeking out of the bag and everyone knowing they would go unopened.

The Social Worker stuck her head out the door at 20 minutes past the appointed time. She said, "It looks like she is not coming. I am sorry."

Then she went to shut the door. I asked her if I could speak with her for a few minutes. I had driven for two hours to get here and there was no way I was going to lose this opportunity to express my views.

She said, "Oh I have another appointment," which I knew to be complete bullshit since she had my appointment.

I told her, "I think I deserve a few minutes of your time." She reluctantly acquiesced.

We sat in her cold old office in dirty hard plastic chairs and I explained my thoughts.

I said it was, "cruel to bring me here today." This was a pattern I was living with the courts. Give some hope that the system is working and then at the last minute there was failure and an "Oh well, we tried. Did the best we could. Sorry."

She asked me what I thought she could do and held up her hands.

I told her that she could take the Visitation Document, walk across the hall and change one number: the date. Make the appointment for the 11th of December and then email the document to my wife's attorney.

She did it, almost. She went and got the Judge to change the date but, they could not email Soledad's attorney. She would have to be hand notified. I knew this was never going to happen. I was not going to see my children and give them the presents.

However, I knew I wasn't going to see them from the moment my lawyer told me I was going to see them. It is just too easy to keep the kids from the father.

I did make my stand. The people in the offices were getting to know me. They knew I was a school administrator. They knew I cared. They knew my face and they saw my tears.

I left the office and told the Social Worker I appreciated her time. She said they would try and notify Soledad that afternoon but I knew better than to hope.

I met the Family Court Judge's clerk in the hallway and she said she was sorry I didn't get to see the children. People were seeing me as more than an alleged crazy gringo abuser.

I was becoming human to them. I considered that important, but it wasn't.

Chapter 7: Abuelo's Office.

The next day I drove back to the courthouse and sat in the same chair and I waited. The tears didn't come today. There was no hope from the outset.

The Social Worker peeked her head out the door and told me it looks like my children and Soledad were not notified and would not be coming.

I asked her for just a minute of her time. She was frustrated and curt.

I thanked her for her efforts and told her I hoped she could help my children. I was praying for her and praying for my children.

We said goodbye. She quickly shut the door.

I had achieved my goal. I knew I wasn't going to see my children. I wanted to be present. I wanted people to see me as human and each day as valuable in the lives of my children.

The first day was for tears. The second day visit was just to be present. I wasn't going to bend the ear of anyone. I wasn't going to make them feel bad or cry or make a scene about what a travesty the justice system is. I made my point the day before so I left with my dignity and the bags of presents just a little more rumpled from wear.

I had one last hope to get these presents to the children.

I went to Abuelo's office.

Most every day, Abuelo, who is 93 as of this writing in Sept 2013, takes a bus into San Jose and sits outside the post office in the city center. It was built in the 1890's with plenty of arches and majesty and curved windows and pigeons shitting on everything.

Almost daily, Abuelo goes to the central market and buys bananas and then goes people watching at his "office." He used to have friends that he would meet there and they watched the pretty girls walk by. All his friends are gone but he still goes out of ritual and lack of anything better to do.

The restraining order was clear that I could have no contact with Soledad or her family. I was playing with fire by contacting Abuelo. I spoke with him when I first arrived and asked for his assistance with my family. He said he was too old to help.

We had parted with a hug and a kiss four months before. How would we meet this time? Would he call the police?

During the Domestic Violence hearing my wife said that her grandparents were so afraid that I would visit them that they had to put new, bigger locks on their doors.

I entered the paved shaded area in front of the post office. There are office workers smoking cigarettes and lottery ticket salespeople calling out the numbers of the winning tickets they are selling. School children with backpacks bouncing, rush across the square in a hurry to leave or get to an education, old folk sit and look at nothing and that is where I found Abuelo.

He greeted me with a big hug. He said I looked great. The last time I saw him he said I looked fat. He does not pull punches. He has one of the few luxuries of 94 years: He doesn't give a shite about what he says to anyone.

We sat down and I asked about Abuela. He said he had not seen Sean, Ted and Elizabeth in a while. I briefed him on the meeting in the courthouse to visit with the children and the failure of the courts to allow me to be a father.

I asked him about the locks on the house. Was there ever a time when he was afraid? He laughed out loud. He put his arm around me and laughed some more. "No, John, I was never afraid of you." He brushed it off as a joke and told me not to worry.

I told him that I didn't think it was true but that is what Soledad stated to the court and the judge wasn't laughing. The judge didn't think it was funny at all that old folk in their 90's had to double lock the doors for fear of the crazy gringo intruder.

I asked him if he would consider delivering my Christmas presents to the children.

I started to take the name tags off the presents that said, "From Papá," but he told me to stop that. The children should know where the presents came from.

I love that man.

He took the presents and we hugged and kissed. I never knew my grandfathers but I imagine them like Don Eduardo Garcia as he turned and walked away from me that day. He was tough and proud and not afraid of lies or the truth.

It was been two years since I saw him and I doubt we will meet again in this life.

God Bless Abuelo.

"Holy Mary, Mother of God, pray for us sinners…"

Chapter 8: Welcome to the Machine.

When I requested visits at the end of June 2011, I entered into the Costa Rican Justice System. I figured I would see my children in three weeks, a month and an outside shot that I could be kept away for more than a month. I was wrong.

This is the tension that I was living: I could neither see nor speak with my children. I was obligated to pay child support but could not work legally in the country. I was also not free to leave the country. If I tried to leave, I would be detained at the airport. Finally, I had to deposit money into the State Approved bank account every month but, since my Visa had expired, I could not legally deposit money.

To renew the Visa, to be able to legally deposit money, I would have to leave the country, but I couldn't leave the country.

These are the silly objective facts.

In theatre, this would be a comedy but I wasn't laughing yet.

Our Domestic Violence hearing was on September 7, 2011. I was waiting for an appointment with the Psychologist; the appointment was scheduled for mid-March 2012. For these five months there would be no contact with my children. Any attempt at contact would be met with a strong and prompt police presence in my world. They would arrest me first and ask questions later.

I waited out the five months to March, I have described the little torture session at Christmas where I was supposed to see the children but that rug was yanked and my tears spilled.

In January, a Social Worker with whom I had already had a three hour interview came to visit me in Jaco. We sat in my small neat apartment and she asked me, "Who does the cooking?"

Then she looked at the iron and asked me, "Who did the ironing?" I kept my smiley face on and told her that I ironed my own clothes. I was wearing my ironed school clothes at the time.

I had already told her that when I lived with my wife that I did all the washing for five, I ironed my own clothes, cooked, did all the major food shopping, cleaned the bathrooms, vacuumed and did most of the dishes.

I offered to cook her lunch.

We had a pleasant visit but her questions about who cooked for me and who ironed for me stuck me as far afield. I was not being understood in the least. She still saw me as the "Useless Husband" and the "Crazy Gringo." It is tough to shake a stereotype.

I continued to teach teachers and help students at my school. I developed a culture of communication between parents and improved the level of English on a school wide basis. I was responsible for 170 students but was unable to see or speak with my own.

"Hail Mary Full of Grace...."

Chapter 9: Psychologist Interview.

In March, I was finally interviewed by the Psychologist. Her office was windowless, humorless, plantless, and merciless. The 1970's office chairs screeched raw metal on poured concrete floors that punctuated slight body shifts into uncomfortable moments. Shifting in the chair to settle yer' balls sounded like the factory floor of a machine shop or a slaughterhouse with heart searing, high pitched porcine cries.

The meeting lasted for two hours.

She began the interview by telling me at length that "in her office" fathers have the same rights as mothers and that there is no favoritism towards women. She was a used car salesman telling me I could trust *her*, but not anyone else involved in the process. She made it sound as if her office operates in a vacuum of equality which only highlighted the shortcomings of the other offices involved in the Family Court System. Maybe in her office fathers have equal rights, but inside her office only represents 5% of the system.

Women hold power in the Family, Domestic Violence, and Child Support Courts. Fathers are not highly undervalued; fathers are not valued at all. Equal rights are not shared between couples in the Family Court. I thought at the time that the system was plum until she implicated the inequality of the other offices by insisting on the impartiality of her part in the system.

I started from the beginning with my story and I left nothing out. My lawyer told me to lie. She said, "Do not mention that you ever smoked marijuana." Lie.

My lawyer was adamant on this point. She threatened to abandon the case if I would not help myself by lying. If I wasn't willing to lie, then she wouldn't be held responsible for the outcome. She was a real negotiating strategist. It was late in the game for me to get another lawyer and I didn't have the funds to hire one anyway.

The only lie I told was when I told my lawyer I would lie.

I wouldn't lie or stretch the truth. I said that I had smoked marijuana infrequently. I didn't smoke around the children. I gave up smoking marijuana when my wife asked me and for that matter I had also giving up smoking cigarettes, like my wife requested of me. My children had never seen me smoke anything. I also mentioned that when we met, my wife smoked more marijuana than I did. Marijuana in our lives was not a cult secret.

I should have just lied and said I never smoked. I lie and she lies and we all lie together, but I didn't and it most likely had a negative affect…it couldn't have helped. I took drugs tests the first few months in Costa Rica and then I took tests before any hearing or meeting. All the tests were clean of marijuana, cocaine and barbiturates (whatever they are).

I cried three or four times throughout the two hour interview. The lady psychologist sat and took notes. She was a good listener. She seemed sympathetic. She was pleased to tell me that I would have four supervised visits and that the Family Court was going to notify my wife when she brought in the children for their psychology appointments.

My children had their father removed from their lives without explanation. They had not heard from me for 8 months and now they were going to have to come into the courthouse and be interviewed by a strange person.

I told the Psychologist that the children deserved consistency so as not to cause more harm. I hoped that after the 4 visits I wouldn't be cut off from the children again for another 8 months…10 months. The children needed a vision for the future.

The Psychologist couldn't tell me that my communication with the children would be established on a consistent basis. I asked if we could both agree that my children need consistency in their lives, that if the court is willing to reintroduce me into their lives that I shouldn't get yanked out capriciously. She agreed that introducing me and then removing me without a plan would have a negative affect but she was powerless to do anything. She raised her hands like Pilate, refusing any responsibility for the travesty that was occurring.

We were all just cogs in a dysfunctional system and that is not any good. I started considering how to get out of the system.

Eight months in the country and my wife and I had yet to sit in the same room together. What we needed was communication. The lawyers were still pissing at each other and not calling back. There was no communication between the lawyers, no communication between my wife and me and no communication between my children and their father, which is exactly how my wife wanted things, that, and the money.

I pleaded with the psychologist that from all of these proceedings what my wife and I needed was to communicate. Could there be a mediator who could sit in the same room with my wife and me to facilitate communication? Without communication how could we possibly be expected to improve our situation so as to be equitable for all involved?

The children had a father who was ready, willing and able and yet I was sidelined, muted and invisible.

Outside the psychologist's office the assistant to the Family Court Judge, Julia, approached me. Julia and the judge both knew me on sight from my frequent visits to the Family Court.

Julia told me that I had been granted 4 supervised visits of fifty minutes each, in the courthouse with my children. I would be able to see and speak with the children.

Julia told me that since the court system could not notify my wife at her house, that Julia would notify Soledad when she came to the courthouse for her Psychologist meeting. Julia would notify my wife personally. She promised she would not miss the chance.

Character is revealed over time. I was gaining sympathies with the family court personnel. They knew how some women work the system and this was Julia's way of tipping the scales of justice to a more equitable level.

I thanked Julia.

It felt like a small success.

I had visits scheduled with the children.

There was a hearing in the Family Court for June. Three more months and we would both be sitting in front of a judge and the lies and the truths would be revealed. My children and I would be granted our rights.

That is what I thought that day leaving the Psychologist's office. I had hope and like all my other hopes, this was a false hope.

That psychologist wouldn't file her report for 6 months. All toll, the Psychologist cost me a year without my children….6 months to wait for the appointment and 6 months for her to write the report.

My wife would fail to appear to the Family Court Hearing, yet the Judge waited 5 months to write his decision…but I am jumping ahead.

At the time, I had hope, so I lived day to day, in the presence of children not my own, and night by night, sleeping under the safety of a strong bright light.

"Hail Mary full of grace…"

*During the course of the 18 months that I was in Costa Rica Dan Knight was sending Soledad money, paying for her plane tickets, living with my children and paying for everything when he was there. I was also paying monthly child support. Soledad had almost everything she wanted. Me out, Dan part-time and both of us providing funding.

Chapter 10: Supervised Visits.

After 10 months in Costa Rica my children were granted four Supervised Visits in the Social Services Department of the San Jose Courthouse.

I prepared for the meeting with gifts of clothes and essentials: toothbrushes and socks, books and pencils, sneakers and sweatshirts. I arrived at the courthouse with a large duffle bag filled with my Father Wares to make the meeting as comfortable as possible. The secretary was confused about the bag and I had to show her what I brought with me.

I paced the hallway hoping for a glimpse of my children. I saw them enter: my wife, three children and my father-in-law. Sean ran to me and I picked him-up. We both began crying. I held Ted to my legs. Soledad clutched Elizabeth.

I asked, "So what do we do now?"

My wife, with an anger I was used to, said, "You should be where you are supposed to be," with that, I put Sean down and she ushered the children down a side hallway.

Turns out there are two doors to enter the department. Nobody told me, but my wife had assumed the worst and let me know about her disdain. Nothing had improved; I expected some light from the tunnel of her emotions and hate towards me. It was an all-black tunnel, a room with no windows, just like the one we were about to enter.

I went round to the opposite door and waited to be led into the Visitation Room. The psychologist who would be observing laid out the ground rules. I must speak in Spanish, English was strictly prohibited. I told the Psychologist (in Spanish) that the children and I had never spoken in Spanish to each other and that Spanish would do nothing but hinder our already broken communication.

She told me in no uncertain terms that English was prohibited and that the session would terminate if I spoke to the children in English.

Sean and Ted came in and we hugged and hugged and held each other. They were confused. They hadn't seen me in almost a year and now we were stuck in a small room being observed by other people.

Elizabeth did not want to leave her mother. She had just woken up from a nap and was crying and holding on to Soledad. I said to Soledad, "You can hold her. Sit in here or go out to the other room. The most important thing is that Elizabeth is comfortable."

Sean, Ted and I sat down on their blankets for a family meeting which I have described in a previous chapter.

We all took our shoes and socks off. They showed me new teeth and wiggly teeth. I checked Sean's crooked toe and taped it into correct position. I gave him the tape to take home.

We ate their favorite foods.

About 10 minutes into the meeting, Elizabeth came in to see her brothers and her father. At the time Sean was 7, Ted was 5 (with a birthday coming in a few weeks) and Elizabeth was 2 years, 6 months.

We started opening presents. I bought angel wings for Elizabeth and a Barbie beauty set. Elizabeth let me brush her hair. We washed our hands, ate and then sat to read a book.

We hugged and talked and played. It was like we did not miss a beat.

These were the children who were supposed to be afraid of me?

I kept time and gave the countdown at 10 minutes so no one was surprised when it was time to leave.

We cleaned up and hugged goodbye. I told the boys that we would see each other in a week. I gave them a calendar and marked the days when we had scheduled meetings.

When Soledad took the children into the hallway, they banged on the smoky glass windows, and yelled, "Bye-bye Papá, bye-bye Papá!"

I could see their amorphous outline in the smoky glass. They were shadows to me and I to them. We had our connection but the reality was all smoky glass and mirrors.

I sat on a child's sized chair, my knees to my chest and wailed, deep choking gasps of sadness escaped. I had always cried silently, even when Sean was diagnosed with cancer, the tears were noiseless. Now that I had seen my children again, the pain washed over me and was released in loud visceral aaaahhhhhh, ahhhaaaaaaaahhha ….aaahaaaaahaaaaaahaaaa….aaaaaaaaahaaaaaaaaahaaaaaa.

The howling.

I didn't know people could cry like that. If I had seen those tears in a movie I may not have believed the actor.

Salt found salt, my tears mixed with sweat. I was removed from my children again. Seemed like nobody cared. The psychologist however, was real anxious, it was 4:35 and her day officially ended at 4:30pm.

I hurried-up, packed, and walked out crying and praying.

"…*Mother of God, pray for us sinners.*"

Chapter 11: Sleeping with the Light On.

I drove the two hours home, in silence. I was traumatized. I didn't go to work the next day. I was sick and scared and alone. I stayed in the house, curtains closed. I read and wrote and prayed.

Elizabeth's hair was messy and her shirt was too small and soiled.

Sean's shorts were too small and his sneakers were worn.

Ted was busting out of his shirt and he needed a haircut.

The beautiful life we left was replaced with unkempt kids and a five year old worried if, "I made a lot of money."

During this time, I started sleeping with the light on, a spotlight with a 100 watt bulb that I would edge in close to. Nightmares had bullied me for over a year, but now I was more desperate and trying to cope. I found that if I left the light on, then the bad dreams wouldn't come so much. I felt a connection to Ted when I left the light on. I can't explain why this connected me to my son, he wasn't afraid of the dark, only his dad was.

I felt great peace being close to the light. I had arrived at a place of honesty, I was without shame. Nothing could touch me as profoundly as the pain that I was feeling by being refused access to my children.

For our anniversaries and birthdays I gave my wife lamps: the gift of light. Beauty is a question of light. Our house shown with the light I had given: Small stained glass lamps or paper machete shades with leaves impressed and rough hemp rope settled around smooth dark wood. I also gave the boys light, lava lamps were our favorite.

I would see the children again next week and I would continue to prepare myself and although I slept with the light on if I slept at all, I knew that soon I would be given my equal share and that the children would have their rights restored.

My children have the right to know their father; it's Article 53 of Constitution of Costa Rica. That book sat on the back of my toilet for a full year. I left it there when I ditched that apartment, that country and that life.

I rarely spoke of my own rights. People don't give a shite about the rights of fathers. When I spoke of the children's rights the spotlight was shifted onto the appropriate subject.

What would I bring for next week's visit? I began to prepare.

*Dan Knight confirmed that Soledad purposefully sent the children to the first meeting in old clothes.

Chapter 12: Second Visit.

Within the first year of their lives, I black brushed the children's feet and imprinted their soles: Black on white on canvas, with their names and age at time of print.

I bought another canvas for each of us to place our hands on at the next Supervised Visit. It was the 7th of March 2012.

For our second visit, I was equally prepared and loaded for bear. After seeing the state of the children's sneakers I bought two new pairs of Nike trainers. They were the sneakers I wanted as a child but never had.

I wrote my phone number in permanent marker on the bottom of the shoes insert.

I brought pictures of myself and pictures of us together.

Pizza and plantains (Teddy's favorite), Doritos and chocolate, water and strawberries, wet wipes and hand sanitizer, clothes, balls, race cars and a green chenille frog faced pillow for Elizabeth.

We met in the same room with blankets spread and food laid out.

We met with huge hugs and Elizabeth came right into the room. We had a family meeting and made our handprints on canvas. When we were washing hands afterwards, Sean said, "Papá these are like our baby footprints." I was touched that he remembered as the black swirled down the drain reminding me that some things are gone forever but that a power exists in storing the memories.

This book is a storage bin of family memories. I knew things could never be the same but if I could just have contact with my children, I could live with the rest.

My best case scenario was having access to the children 3 times a week and every other weekend. I did not yet understand the worst case scenario. The worst case scenario has passed…that I would not see the children for another year; that I would be arrested and face jail time. Fortunately, I didn't have any idea of what a worst case scenario looked like.

During the second meeting, two other events occurred that were of note.

Ted began drawing on the whiteboard. His first drawing was a picture of me. I was brushing Elizabeth's hair and Ted said, "Look Papá, I made a picture of you."

I sent a mental message to the Psychologist sitting behind me taking notes that Ted's picture spoke volumes on my connection with him. I was smiling in the picture.

At about this time Elizabeth was in my arms. She took her cues from the boys and since they were 100% cool, she was 100% cool.

She called me, "Papá" for the first time in the meetings.

It was another significant step in the process and I am certain the Psychologist noted this transition. The moment is in the minutes of the meetings.

These were the children who were supposedly afraid of me. In the final report of the meetings it is mentioned no less than 15 times that the children, "Showed no fear."

"No kidding," I thought. We could have established that with a 15 minute meeting with the judge. Instead my children went without a father for over a year.

"Hail Mary, full of grace…"

Chapter 13: Number of Days.

At the third meeting, my lawyer requested more visits. We were granted two more visits for a total of 6. I asked the psychologist the plan for after those visits. She told me that there are limited resources and there was no plan. I would most likely have to wait for the Family Court hearing, which means I would again be removed from my children's lives without a definitive plan to continue communication.

I realized then that the purpose of the visits was not to re-initiate contact with my children; the purpose of the visits was to produce a document that would end with a recommendation for the judge.

We continued our visits. In our last family meeting, I could give no answers to my children's questions: When will we see you again? When can you call us?

Nothing...a blank slate handed down from the courts to me and then from me to my children. We hugged and we kissed and that is the last time I touched my children....the date was April 25, 2012.

Like all the other poignant moments in this journey, "I didn't know it at the time," that that meeting would be our last with no others in the future.

I still had hope on that day, it is no longer sad to me, even in retrospect. I look back on the fool who I was and the man that I am and every decision I made that has lead me to this day: 26 September 2013 and a new number in my head: 520: The number of days since I last saw or spoke with my children.

I expected a court hearing in June, so I prepared for a month without the children until the judge would finally hear our case. The court case in June would mark one year in the country. I felt closer to the end of the long tunnel, from the distance, what I thought was the light at the end turned out to be a firefly just a few yards ahead of me. The reality is that the path has been long and dark forever since.

Life is grand otherwise, I am wildly in love with a woman who wildly loves me, my career is upturning and I have nearly produced a book: the dream of my life. I am in the best physical shape of my life. I live two blocks from the beach and watch every sunset.

I well appreciate what the universe has given but I am still in a dark tunnel without my children while my spiritual development moves forward towards the light.

The light are my children whom I last saw 44,814,600 seconds, 747,360 minutes, 12,456 hours, 520 days or 74 weeks ago.

Every parent eventually has to let go of their children. My time came sooner than I expected and not of my own choice nor the decision of my children.

"Dear Lord please help my daughter Elizabeth."

Chapter 14: Positive Reports.

The Sociologist conclusion after a two hour interview in San Jose, a visit to my apartment at the beach and several unofficial meetings:

Parental Rights of John P. Murphy should be restored.

The report from the Psychologist Office of 6 Supervised visits where every spoken word was written:

Parental Rights of John P. Murphy should be restored.

I was standing at the finish line, waiting for the road crew to hold up the tape so I could break on through and be a father to my children.

Redeemed. Restored. Justice?

Chapter 15: Mediation.

The day before the Family Court audience with the judge, my wife and our lawyers will meet in the judge's chambers and see if we can hammer out a reasonable deal. I was optimistic after reading the reports. I was armed with a clean drug test in hand in case those accusations reappeared.

With some luck, I will see my children in just a few days, or maybe it will take three weeks for the paperwork, or there is an outside shot it will take three months for everything to clear.

I had been a 3-3-3 man for one full year, but I was getting closer.

Mediation appointment is set for 1pm.

By 1:30pm my wife is declared a, "No-show." There was no phone call, no message from her attorney, nothing. That type of behavior gets you fired from McDonald's.

Go home. Come back tomorrow for the hearing.

I spoke with my attorney and we felt that my wife's failure to appear probably won't work to her benefit. It shows unwillingness to compromise and disrespect for the courts.

Right?

"Dear Lord, Jesus Christ, please help my son Ted."

Chapter 16: Trial Day.

The Family Court audience with the judge arrived on 6 June 2012. It was time to prove allegations as false and be restored as father to Sean, Ted and Elizabeth. I was sitting at the table for a year, starving, while waiting for justice to be served. I could have my rights restored by day's end. Positive reports all around.

I stayed in San Jose that night. I slept little. I left the light on.

At 9:00am I sat with my attorney and Don Roberto, who came as a character witness. He is a friend and a lawyer who advised me from the beginning. He is a sharp, polite, well-mannered, successful lawyer. He has been around the block and carries confidence and mental acuity like most carry a wallet. Even the judged couldn't help admiring Don Roberto.

By 9:30am we were still waiting for my wife. The judge came out of his office and asked us to join him to begin the testimony.

My wife was again a "No Show," for my opportunity to present my case.

I felt like this was not the person I married. That Soledad would disregard the courts was unthinkable to me. The idea that she would fail to attend a court appearance blew my mind. We were in this court for a year and she had used every option to extend the process to its limits.

Hundreds of work hours and lots of money had been invested in this process and after a year of waiting: no show. She had wasted the time and effort of the courts by not respecting the process by appearing.

"Smite this behavior. Smite it!" was the phrase ringing in my mind. Smite non-compliance and reward diligence for the benefit of my children.

We presented my testimony and the judge said that we would wait until after lunch for my wife to arrive. She was not required to be present for my testimony.

My testimony ended by 11am and I went to lunch alone.

The feeling was that my rights could be granted after lunch. If my wife did not show up, the judge could immediately grant visitation.

I will be restored, redeemed. I will be able to speak with my children and hug them and go to their schools and call them on the phone.

I was minutes away from that decision.

After lunch my wife was still a, "no show." No word from her attorney. Nothing.

So, I won, right?

Chapter 17: No Show. I Win?

The judge came into the hallway at 1:30pm and said that he wouldn't wait any longer for my wife.

Thinking we were chummy now since I was the only one who showed the courts an ounce of respect, I asked when we may have a decision.

The judge said that a report was missing from the Psychologist. "No, no, no." I said, the visits are reported.

He corrected me that there is another report, apart from the visits, that the psychologist must file.

I asked the judge when I would get the opportunity to discount my wife's allegations and the letter from a psychologist from Ted's school that stated I arrived at the school with a "strong odor of marijuana."

The fact that the statement exists in any document is unjust. I wanted the opportunity to discount the accusation and put that to bed.

He said, "Have your attorney explain it" and left. You can say anything you want in the Family Court petition documents because if you don't show up for the hearing you never have to prove your statements nor does the opposing party have the opportunity to discount them, but the judge still reads them.

Again, I suffered colossal disappointment. My three days, three weeks, three months style of living was just extended. I wouldn't see the children in three days, that much was certain.

But I had won right? She didn't show-up. None of her statements had been validated.

Chapter 18: Intimidation.

Right after the Family Court Hearing, but before any decision was made. I received an email from "BigTimeCoward@yahoo.com." I was fairly surprised that the email address was still available in 2012.

I am reprinting the email in its entirety:

"Cowards Die Many Times Before Their Deaths."
William Shakespeare, Julius Caesar

"Cowards can never be moral."
Gandhi

YOU ARE A COWARD!

What "so called" man tries to starve his kids to make a woman who despises him come back?

You have made this very easy!
Your immoral and illegal actions have exposed you to, but not limited to, the following;
US Federal & State Tax fraud (3 counts).
US Federal, State & Local Tax evasion (2 counts each).
Conspiracy to commit US Federal, State & Local Tax evasion & Tax Fraud.
Forgery
Civil Rights violations (against your kids)
Medicaid Fraud
Conspiracy to commit Medicaid Fraud.
PA State Unemployment fraud (btw..There is no statute of limitations here...the other times you have done this have been reported as well).
US Federal Unemployment fraud.
...and conspiracy to commit in BOTH cases.

Your assertion that your "attorneys" have been contacting the petitioner's attorneys is laughable!

Your mom will soon be indicted for....etc. etc.
There is NO stopping this...

The PA house will soon be confiscated by the authorities.

...(you should have been more careful about your emails).

The best part is....these are all committed and provable beyond a reasonable doubt in ALL cases by a preponderance of evidence that you yourself have provided.

Your personal journal has provided me a fabulous insight on your pedophile mind.
Which brings me to the 8 affidavits I have from children you have molested.
Yes....your pedophilia will now be exposed too.
Assuredly you will spend the rest of your life behind bars and certainly NEVER be allowed around Sean (who HATES you), Ted (Who is afraid of you) and H (Who doesn't KNOW you and who also HATES you and is terrified of you).

However, before you get too confident that this is all I found out about you.....while you we're having sex with 14 year old boys and 15 year old girls at the Putaria in Jaco....selling and using drugs (I have great photos)...the above mentioned are class b and c offenses compared to the mother of all offenses (x4) I have on you.

Everything is in the works and as of Friday June 15th at 13:00....all information and supporting documents have been released to the appropriate authorities (who were already briefed and waiting for the documentation)....in fact, they were all instrumental in pulling this all together!
Welcome to the road to PRISON!

..and the only one you have to blame is YOURSELF!
Much Much love.......

The first thought as I read was, "someone is coming to kill me." That heavy Shakespeare quote got me thinking about locking the door.

And then it rambled, it was all over the place. Overkill, the email threatens my mom, I am accused of drug dealing and pedophilia and "the mother of all offenses (x4)."

My only guess for the "mother of all offenses," is murder.

I wasn't worried about the mother of all offenses so much as false accusations of pedophilia. If you are going to lie about someone, that is a nasty one to tell.

I have given professional development to male teachers on methods to avoid accusations of sexual impropriety, because the accusation itself will affect your career. I lived advice that was given to me: Never be alone with a student and never touch a student. I also never texted students and any email contact was copied to parents.

The tricky piece of sexual impropriety is that if you live by the rule: never alone, never touch; you will most likely avoid conviction but you will assuredly be inconvenienced.

If this BigTimeCoward person were willing to send an email to my school, anonymously claiming that I engaged in inappropriate behavior with a child, the school would have no choice but to suspend me until an investigation was completed. Being investigated for Inappropriate Behavior essentially ends that job. Parents are informed there is an investigation and that is that. The world always needs more bartenders.

I showed these emails to few people at the time. I am free now, and not concerned with bullshit accusations, so I print it here to illustrate the insanity of my situation. I had a Restraining Order against me and now this goofball is accusing me of pedophilia and the "mother of all offenses." And they kidnapped my children.

Aside from each of the allegations being a bluff, what made me laugh was the rambling soap opera style writing and the "Who Done It" cadence.

None of the allegations are true, so I let it go, except that part about how I, "should have been more careful with my email."

That stuck in my mind.

*Dan Knight confirmed that Soledad wrote the BigTimeCoward emails.

Chapter 19: Keylogger.

I had heard the term years before but the music didn't start to play until that last wacky email. I assumed my wife had used, stolen or somehow knew my password for my email but I had changed it more than once, I had also changed my Yahoo settings, I found my wife's email listed to receive messages with admin privileges.

I started looking on my computers hard drives for the names of programs that were unfamiliar and I started uninstalling programs. A window popped up on the screen, I don't know what I did to make it appear but there were the words that I was looking for: "Keyloggerexe."

A keylogger is a program uploaded to a computer that transfers every keystroke of the infected computer to a second computer. I took my laptop to one of the computer experts who hangs at my buddy Steve's hardware store. He told me he would clean the computer professionally.

When he finished, he told me the hacker performed an amateur job, uploading three different Free Keylogger programs until one worked. My computer had been tapped since February of 2010.

I can't prove my wife uploaded the keylogger, although she was the only person with access to my computer, I didn't take it to school, it sat on my desk, in my office at home, but that is not the point, the point is that I was ignorant to the type of relationship I had with my wife. I believe so strongly in personal privacy, no one had to teach me that reading documents that were not meant for you is wrong. I considered that some kind of inalienable right only broken by spies and politician's helpers.

I remember sending my brother an email saying, "I should just fly down to Costa Rica, pick-up the kids and go right to the Embassy."

In another email I wrote, "Man, if this keeps up I will leave her in 2026 when Elizabeth turns 18."

Now, the chances of me stealing my children from my wife are virtually non-existent. I wouldn't steal my children from their mother. It would pain my children and it is selfish. I wrote that scenario as a non-viable option.

My wife read it as a threat and she acted according to what her imagination of the future told her was going to happen. She wasn't supposed to read that. It wasn't to her and it affected her decisions and since she was planning on kidnapping the children, she assumed that I was capable of the same.

Every thief judges from their own disposition.

I wasn't worried about the keylogger. I had nothing to hide. I hadn't cheated on my wife nor engaged in illegal activity and had nothing to be embarrassed about.

What did concern me was that if she could take information off of my computer, could she put information on my computer?

I never got the answer to that question and to date I have had nothing incriminating appear on my computer. Thank God for favors.

I expected to be given my rights to the children in 3 days, 3 weeks or 3 months.

Chapter 20: 3/3/3.

The Family Court hearing was June 6. Three days, three weeks, three months. Still, I live this torture of, "When will I see my children."

The Domestic Violence Restraining Order expired of its one year enforcement on September 7.

Ok, so my wife didn't show-up for the Family Court Hearing and all the reports are favorable. The court will wait until the day the Restraining Order expires then the psychologist hands in her report, the judge makes his decision and we move on. Sharpish like.

Just wait a couple more months John and it will all be over in a day.

I wanted to scream and pull out the hair that I don't have. Two more months without my children and they have no idea where I am or what is happening. They were kidnapped for two more months.

I had no choice. My attorney advised me to do nothing. Any attempt to push the judge or the psychologist could be construed as me trying to pressure them or me trying to "tell them how to do their job." People don't like being told how to do their job. I get that.

I went to the courts anyway, just once.

Hoping.

Chapter 21: Restraining Order Ends.

The Restraining Order ended without a sound. One day it was there and the next it did not apply. Or did it?

The sticky wicket about Restraining Orders is that once they expire it only takes a phone call or email to have the Restraining Order Re-Instated. If my wife complained, I would again be removed from my children for another year. If the first Judge thought it fit enough to restrain a person the second Judge is not going to do anything different.

My wife had been lying to me and about me for a couple a years at this point. Why wouldn't she lie again?

I had sent an email to my wife after the third meeting with the children. I thought that we were getting over the hump and that I was being re-instated in the lives of my children.

In the Restraining Order it says that I cannot, "threaten or perturb" the plaintiff.

I sent my wife the following email after 9 months of no contact. I thought that it could never be construed as threatening. I was testing the waters.

Here is the email in its entirety followed by the response I received from "Antonio" via my wife's email:

Hi Soledad,

I hope this finds you well.

Sean has been missing that front tooth for the 3 weeks I have seen him. He told me it fell out months ago.

If the tooth does not start coming in during three weeks it means that he needs to go to the dentist so the dentist can cut the gum.

Will you take him to the dentist?

If you care to discuss this you can give me a call.

My cell phone is 5701-2221.

I wish nothing but the best for you.

Sincerely,

John

For me that email was innocuous. I was a concerned father attempting to communicate with my wife over issues that concerned the health of our child. No big whoop. I was testing the water.

The water was really cold.

Here is the Response I received:

John,

You are in violation of your restriction/ non-contact order from the Domestic Violence Case that you were proven guilty in.

Cease and desist contacting Soledad now or face the full weight of the law.

No contact means:
1. NO contact.
2. NO emails!
3. NO threatening phone calls!
4. NO conversations!

All of which you have done or made.

Your manipulation and intimidation games are over!

I know you think you are a pretty smart guy, but I suggest if you were, you wouldn't have left such an easy trail to follow. You have exposed yourself and I intend to expose you!

You are dealing with me now and I have a ZERO tolerance policy.

Furthermore, I intend to expose every illegal activity you have been and currently are involved in.

The U.S., Costa Rican and International laws you have broken and violated are enough to put you away for life.
You have already given me ample proof and I have been in contact with and provided it to the proper local, state and government authorities in both both countries.

Again, Cease and desist ANY contact with Soledad or this time we will not hesitate to have the police throw you in Jail where you belong for the numerous violations

Antonio

Chapter 22: Big Time Coward.

A person can complain about any contact. Now, I even have this third party threatening me. And Antonio said he has a, "Zero Tolerance Policy," a real tough one I hear.

That Zero Tolerance line still makes me laugh.

My children had been taken away from me over a year ago and this guy is threatening me his Zero Tolerance Policy.

So although the Restraining Order ended, I couldn't call my children or go to their school. I couldn't email my wife. My family couldn't call the children. Any attempt my family made to contact the children was putting a favorable decision for me at-risk.

My wife could complain that my family was harassing her.

I toed that line.

Three days, three months, three weeks, which one will it be? I lived with the unknowing and the bright expectation that I was now past the middle of the journey. I was surely closer to my children than I was away from them.

But I was close. I could feel it.

While I bided my time for the Restraining Order to expire I received a few more emails from BigTimeCoward.

In fact, I recall turning on my computer one Saturday morning and thinking, "I haven't heard from BigTimeCoward in a few weeks. Maybe BigTimeCoward was alone and drunk on a Friday night and decided to throw around the old bull after a few glasses of wine."

And sure enough, I received the following:

"Faced with what is right, to leave it undone shows a lack of courage."
-Confucius

"Those who lack courage, by default, are COWARDS!"
-Anonymous

FYI, putting your house up for sale DOES NOT in any way undue what you have done.

There are no statutes of limitations for many of your actions, or the statutes will not be exceeded for at least another 5 years.

The LONG ARM of the Law is reaching for you!

Do the right thing!

Or choose the consequences of your actions which include, but are not limited to:

1. Exposing your mother and landing her in prison.
2. Extend your stay in prison, beyond what you will already be doing time for.

Child endangerment and pedifilia are serious crimes which are elevated to hate crimes given your published racist views.

Much Much Love!

Then another email arrived a few days later:

Hey Chester,

...your freedom.....

can you feel it slipping away?

You made some BIG boo-boos....and the boys are talking.

You are a SICK SICK person!

What made you do it?
The drugs?
Or were you projecting?

Did you think it wouldn't come out?

Are you that arrogant?
Or delusional?

You know your profile matches perfectly with that of a pediphile.....
...once it was exposed...people starting seeing it bright as day.

Everyone is singing like canaries....even Billy.

However, I'm sure he will deny it!
You see...he didn't want to be exposed.

Don't you hate it when you think you covered your tracks and had good solid allies......and then it all unravels?
Damn it I hate it when that happens!

...the laws a comin boy!
...much much love lol

Part V

The Second Pilgrimage

29 July 2012

Chapter 1: The Pilgrim Revisited.

A year had passed since I completed the first pilgrimage. I still had the message of that first pilgrimage tattooed on my brain. The message lent clarity: Life is pain. Get used to it.

I decided I would walk the Pilgrimage from Jaco to Cartago once again. I was 15 pounds lighter, in peek physical condition from surfing and running. I would knock out the pilgrimage with less pain and suffering than the last. I felt like I could run to Cartago.

I had a powerful relationship with Abuelo.

Abuelo walked on the railroad tracks from Orotina to San Jose. I decided I would follow in his footsteps and see what he saw. The pilgrimage would have new meaning for me; I would make a connection with the past and walk along the mountain top.

I was a pilgrim again. A year older, a year without my children, a year with days and nights of tears and pain and although the end was within sight (I thought), I had little confidence in the system and less confidence that my wife would willingly allow me to see the children when the time came.

She had used all means to slow the process, I was defending against lies and half-truths and quarter lies and at no point was there a lessening of her disdain for me. I feared that if she was willing to lie once, what would stop her from lying again?

The thought of the first possible visit with my children scared me. My wife could say I came to the house smelling like marijuana. She could protest at any moment and I would again be stripped of my rights and the process would start anew.

What if Ted fell on our first visit? What if Elizabeth cried for any reason?

When frivolous fears and unaccountable lies are treated as the Buddha cow by the justice system, there is no "over the limit" on the Bullshit Breathalyzer. Every inebriated fecal statement flowing into the courts is permitted past the checkpoint of validity to slaughter roadside innocents. Great turds of falsehood travel the system, going around ninety, driving 54 Packard's. They crash, in head-on accidents where nobody hits the brakes, against Psychologists on unicycles, and judges tapping canes on the sidewalk.

Experienced lawyers see these drunken lies for what they are and prepare accordingly, you will never see an experienced lawyer, like the fellow I consulted in Pennsylvania, with shite on his suit from the lies of any client, but those young lawyers are covered in the bullshit and flattened by the lies, lawyers who treat you based on the warped fiction they read, where you are the star of the daytime domestic violence drama, like my third lawyer did.

The judges, clerks and psychologists are covered in bullshit but from years of use, they don't care anymore, whatever lies enter the system are passed on, they simply push the shitty paper to the next person in line. There is no progress, only the next day in the life of a government worker.

All it takes is one new accusation from my wife and the wheels stop turning and the process is reset. It was a precarious situation I found myself in and I set off on the second pilgrimage from Jaco with these thoughts in mind.

Chapter 2: Sleeping on the Side of the Road.

The Saturday morning was sunny. The previous year I set out at 10am, a late start for sure, but I had made the walk to Orotina. I set out before 10am on this journey.

The temperature was in the mid-nineties and the sun blazed. I was soaked through after 30 minutes of walking, although I was strong and healthy, this did not look good.

After 90 minutes of walking, I made my bed by the roadside, smashing down weeds to alert snakes, then lay down.

I slept.

I always wondered how people could sleep by the roadside. In Costa Rica, it is not uncommon to see folk sleeping peacefully in an unusual spot. I was now one of those people. The heat and the sweating had wiped me out and my body shut down.

I prayed when I woke up, picked myself up and started walking again. I passed the familiar spots of the year before and reflected on the year that had passed.

My mind focused on my children and our lives together. I thought this second journey would again prove what I was willing to do for the children. I pushed-on, that sunny morning, knowing what awaited me; I would need to be a real tough guy to finish this walk.

Sean and Ted are tough guys. They have the scars to prove it.

Tough Guys and Scars

We were three boys in the house and two of us were tough guys. I wasn't one of them.

Sean and Ted are both gritty by nature and they have the scars to prove it. My wife told our marriage counselor that I was raising Vikings. I don't know about all that, I never banged the boys on the head or forced Darwinian Spartanism on them. Sean and Ted come from hearty Irish stock. Here are a few of the moments where the child is father to the man.

Sean had twelve tubes connected to his body, running fluids in and sucking fluids out. He was kept alive, at two and a half years old, by this messy jumble of tubular plastic known in the hospital as "spaghetti." Lines left to themselves will secretly coil and tangle in the night.

Ask any fisherman or mountain climber.

The surgery to remove the 11cm by 7cm by 6cm (big as a big man's fist) tumor, left Sean with a scimitar shaped wound extending from the third rib on his right side and moving upwards just off the middle of his back to the top the shoulder blades. The doctor winged him.

The tumor could have pressed on his spin at any time to completely paralyze him; it could have spread out to his bones and kidneys and passed around his body. It didn't. He lived.

None of those terrible scenarios realized themselves. Instead, Sean was left with the scars. There have been no technological advances on removing surgical tape from wounds.

The main wound was long. There was a lot of tape. Sean and I stripped down and sat in the steamy bathroom soaping and rubbing for two hours. We reheated the water as I slowly coaxed the adhesive into separating from my son's delicate sutured skin.

Freedom did not come easy; patience and pain were the only remedy. It took three nights to remove all the tape from the wound.

Finally, the neat stitch work was revealed.

Sean didn't complain throughout his cancer treatment, except that one time and then he never complained again.

We were in the Children's Hospital of Philadelphia (CHOP) and Sean needed to drink some magic poison that attaches itself to cancer cells. The cells then show-up on an MRI. He didn't want to drink the solution. He was only 2 and a half so he was not able to think through this situation logically.

Up until this event and every test and needle afterwards he gave up his arm and would drink anything without discussion. But this time, the first and only time, he was adamant. "No, no, no."

"Listen my son, if you don't drink this, they're gonna stick a tube up your nose and it'll go down yer throat and you'll be forced to drink it."

"No, no, nooooo." Tough little Irish bastard. I like spunk but this was going to end badly for him.

Big Mama Nurse told me the plan. I was to throw my body weight on top of Sean to hold him down, then pin his head between my hands so she could snake the tube up his nose. "Ok coach. Got it," I thought without thinking, as if she had asked me to lean into a Nolan Ryan fastball or take an offensive charge from Shaquille O'Neill.

"Don't let em' get lose," she said like an enthusiastic Coach in Pee-Wee Football.

I did it. I pinned him down, held his head and we were eye to eye. The nurse took the three foot long piece of eighth inch plastic hose and began forcing it up Sean's nose. He yells in wide eyed fear, "No Papá, Papá it hurts!"

And the nurse keeps pushing that hose until it passes his nasal passage and his voice goes funny to a choking sound and now he can't yell but his eyes tell me he is totally confused about the traitorous role his father is playing in this assault.

The nurse injected the poison into the tube and it went directly into Sean's stomach and she gave the tube a steady pull and out it came. He was exhausted, confused and felt betrayed. There was no way that was fair.

That's the way life is. "Everybody takes a beating some time." (A Bronx Tale, 1993)

He didn't complain again and he never refused another treatment because that's the way life is sometimes. You get used to it. Sean internalized the concept, "that's the way life is sometimes" and two years later he appropriately pulled that statement out of his magic hat to the hushed awe of his father and his father's friend.

I'll never forget my participation in the assault on my son.

I am mass of scar tissue from watching my son and the other children of Childhood Cancer wards.

Ted's first scar is a one centimeter slice dividing his left eyebrow. He was cut on a weeknight in the winter when dark and cold rush in and send the sun on her way early. My wife had gone out with my sister and a friend for a rare weeknight outing.

After supper, I was on my back, on the living room floor next to the pale yellow dresser, on which rests the fish tank with its soft water sound and peaceful light.

A son stood on either of me, each making music and swaying.

Sean was holding the guitar like an upright base and plucking away. Ted was on the recorder making shallow notes. Both boys moved to a rhythm and song was in the air. I hummed loud. I felt the full happiness of fatherhood. I adore these moments and felt the blessing of the universe when all was right with the world.

Sean let his hand fall from supporting the guitar in an experiment to balance the instrument upright. The guitar stood momentarily and then slowly tipped to port. It fell in a peaceful whoosh and the head of the guitar hit Ted just above the left eye, where bone is protected by only thin skin. The sharp edge of the wood neatly sliced a one centimeter vertical opening.

"Owe." said Ted.

"Shite" thought I.

The thin line of blood trickled down and I pushed a tissue on the wound. Ted didn't cry or protest.

I called my sister's cell phone with the news and we packed up to go to the hospital which is only a few minutes' drive from the house. Ted held the tissue with aplomb. He was empowered and confident. Everything was fine.

We were like three little Fonzies: "Cool."

At the hospital, Ted sat on the edge of the table, legs dangling, while the nurse looked at the wound. Ted sat silent when she opened the wound to irrigate it. She commented to Ted, "Wow, what a big boy you are. No tears." And then to me, "I can't believe it. He didn't make a sound. He is a real tough guy."

No tears, no protests, no whining or fussing. Ted sat there like a boxer, letting his cut man work. A quick butterfly Band-Aid and we were on our way.

Your first scar, my son, is a cool one. I imagine you sitting years later, with a girl of your own, who loves you. She touches your face and feels the bones of your features. She looks into your eyes and notices the small scar the divides your left eyebrow in two. She asks, "What happened here."

You say, in the voice of a tough guy, who doesn't even know he is tough, but simply expresses a natural state of confidence that need not paint drama, seek approval or court admiration:

"Aah, my first scar. I got that from a guitar."

Sean was sitting on a 2" x 6" board tied into the small shade tree that shades our waterfalled fish pond. The sound of the water and the wind chime hanging above is peaceful music that makes for a contemplative mindset. The sound of the moving water trickling over the small flat rocks emits peace in gentle waves for anyone quiet enough to receive it.

From that perch in the tree, his lifeguard stand, Sean had a Buddha moment. Our neighbor Mike was visiting. Mike and I were standing. The late summer heat on this sunny afternoon had receded.

Mike explained that his job ended abruptly. He had a job and then he didn't. He thought he was going to be able to start on the repairs to his house and now he couldn't. Another sad story of life: He needed money and he needed a job and what he needed at this moment was support from friends. I was that friend and Sean more so.

I didn't know what to say to Mike.

From the perch of the tree, Sean said nothing for the ten minutes while Mike explained his predicament. My son's thin legs dangled and swayed.

He looked at Mike and said, "Well, Mike, that's the way life is sometimes."

I had used that phrase any number of times in explaining life's capricious nature. Sean internalized that meaning and used that phrase without guile or sentiment and passed the advice on to my friend.

Mike looked and said, "You got that right Sean."

There were two tough guys in my house and I wasn't one of them.

Chapter 3: Prancing Horse Tears.

I prayed. I walked. I sweated. I was running through two liters of water every hour. Water went in and water seeped out and soaked my shirt, my shorts, and my socks. My body was a filter.

I learned the topography of Costa Rica on these walks more than anything that school or teaching ever taught me. The topography works like this: walk up a mountain and down a mountain, cross a river, walk up a mountain and down and mountain and cross another river.

I kept marching uphill until I arrived at my favorite restaurant. It is an open air rustic Costa Rican version of a diner, pinched between the road and a mountain drop off.

There are twenty odd, roughhewn wooden tables with benches and a view of the valley. Bunches of onions, plantains and garlic hang from the rafters for storage as much as for show. Heavy-set middle aged Ticas with bandana tied hair, stir large cauldrons of soup and shift massive pots of "Gallo Pinto" – rice and beans with cilantro and onion. Gallo pinto is the typical Costa Rican breakfast accompaniment.

With fresh tortillas, gallo pinto and a couple of running eggs I watched an older cowboy train his high stepping horse in a corral just below the restaurant. The animal was sweating from the unnatural high stepping gait.

Pop had a high-stepping Hackney Pony. The Hackneys trot naturally. The man and horse below were learning to trot. Horses remind me of my father.

I hadn't seen my father in over a year. During that time he was in the hospital twice, both times nearing death, both times I couldn't be by his side. Since I couldn't leave the country, I thought I would never see my father again. I believed I would be absent from my family and my mother during his funeral.

The idea that I would never see my father again was a step in accepting the ramifications of the choices I had made. I accepted this as part of my decision to dedicate my life to being a father to my children. My father accepted that my role in this world was larger now than just being his son, I was also a father and maybe we would meet no more on this earth.

The walk, the horse, the sentimentality all washed over me. I cried into my eggs and thought of the last time I had seen my father.

Pop Cries, November 2010

As far as I know, my father, Joseph Patrick Murphy, Jr. cried for the first time when he was 80. I know it was the first time I ever saw him cry. I sat with my parents in their quiet living room and told them that my wife and children were leaving for Costa Rica in two weeks' time and that I was staying to finish the school year. It was late November. The expression on my parents' faces, the silence that followed and the subsequent conversation allowed me to understand that this course of action would not only affect me.

We went through the obvious arguments…she would never let me see the children again, the justice system in Costa Rica would screw me, my wife is going to harm me and the children, followed by a myriad of other points trying to dissuade me from this decision that would harm us all.

Everything my parents said to me that day has come to pass.

My father had a particular connection with horses and he passed over 13 grandchildren trying to find just one, male or female, who gave two tosses about horses.

His hope was Teddy. Ted put on his first cowboy boots at two and didn't take them off for two years. He walked tall in black cowboy boots and a diaper. He wore cowboy boots with shorts, with jeans, in summer and in the winter. He ran through one pair and we bought another. To Ted, cowboy boots are like early Corvettes and Johnny Cash's wardrobe, they come in any color, they just have to be black. Teddy was most comfortable in his boots, a white diaper, no shirt, with little boy belly foremost, walking on tiny heals with pointed toes, carrying a warm bottle of milk.

Pop saw those cowboy boots on Teddy and thought it was the coming of the savior. Teddy liked the horses but the horses' hair didn't like Teddy. He is allergic to horse hair. He swells up and gets big and bumpy along the face and neck and only big doses of Benadryl and a long nap can snap his defense system from the harm of horse hair.

"Ok," Pop figured, "Teddy can look like a cowboy but Sean will be one."

Sean loved the horses and the horses respected him. He had a confidence with the horses that I do not have. It is "in the hands" and in the genes. At two and a half years old Pop and Sean hooked horse to cart and Sean had traces in hand. I have a picture of Sean and Pop, just after they knocked over the back gate, Pop smiling under his newsboy cap and wearing denim over flannel. Sean wore red sweatpants and a blue denim jacket with sheepskin hood. Sean's cheeks and face are red and Pop has his arm around the coming of the King. There will be a Murphy who continues with horses.

Pop quietly bought a small saddle.

Pop had secrets and ways with horses that he wanted to pass on, he wanted to feel the connection with his grandchildren. He worked too much his whole life, so the horses were skipping the generation of my siblings and me. We were disinterested, but now Pop was living his second fatherhood and he would handle things differently this time. He didn't have to work two jobs. He could sit with his grandchild on a Saturday and clean the stables and help my son learn the ways of horses and the ways of the people who surround, tend, and nurture the noble beasts.

When Pop was round 20 years old, he had a horse named Dizzy. Dizzy was a crazy horse. No one except Pop could understand the horse....birds of a feather.

There are types of horses like there are types of people. Dizzy was a horse that didn't think. Dizzy let the rider run the show. Some horses have sense: if they are approaching a fence or a wall they slow or stop or turn. Most horses, if they see a person on the ground, will not step on a prostrate person. Compassion is a lovely note in horses.

This common horse sense did not apply to Dizzy. Dizzy would run through a fence; Dizzy would run full gallop into a brick wall or run over a person without prejudice. Apart from blind faith in the decision of the rider, Dizzy was fast. Real Fast. Dizzy could also turn on a dime, from a full gallop Dizzy would jump, swing her rump around and do a 180 and start off on the gallop again.

Dizzy loved that trick and all Pop could do was hold on.

Pop left for the Korean War and Dizzy was left to my mother's care. Since Dizzy was a crazy horse that nobody but Pop could ride and Pop was due to spend the next four years on Guam and the Philippines, my mother sold Dizzy down the road.

Pop didn't mind, horses are to be bought and sold without sentimentality.

Pop came back from the war and was down at the stables around Welsh Road. At a time when a dime bought a hamburger and coke, Pop always carried $100 in his pocket. Pop was an early recycler. Recycling always paid and if you worked long enough and weren't afraid to get dirty, a person could make some money. Pop picked tin on the dump.

He walked up to a horse that was giving a young kid trouble. The teenager couldn't handle the horse and Pop stood and watched for a while like people in the know tend to do. "Let's see what is going to happen here…this could be interesting" he thought. "If that horse begins to kick shite out of the teenager, I'll step in," but for the moment, Pop stood back and observed.

After seeing the frustration grow, Pop said, "Hey, you wanna sell that horse? I'll give you a $100 for her."

The kid jumped at the offer.

Pop said, "Take yer saddle off him but leave the bridle."

Pop jumped on the horse bareback and grabbed a pick-ax handle that was resting against the fence. He cracked that horse once on the top off the head with the pick-ax handle and the horse took off. He galloped straight for 50 yards and Pop pulled that bridle, dug his heels into Dizzy's side and that horse jumped, 180'ed and charged back towards the stable.

The kid's eyes were wide. He was incredulous that someone could mount that horse and do a trick like that. He had never gotten any use from the horse. The horse sat as potential unlimited. Dizzy just needed the right rider; the man with the confidence and experience to mount him. Dizzy didn't trust just anybody. He was majestic with the correct rider, less than useless and more than a little dangerous with everyone else.

A terrible storm at sea will sink the inexperienced captain. The salty captain, with experience and knowledge can handle the deep crests and troughs and belay his ship up and down and up and down like the rhythm of a nursery rhyme. The captain knows the songs of the waves and follows the path of least resistance.

A storm to this captain is an inconvenience. The same storm to me is certain death. It is not a matter of care or effort or willingness to change and learn. One person has it and another person does not, and you can't learn on the job in the middle of a storm. It is too late, you are in over your head and try as you might, the ship is sinking.

My relationship suffered the same.

I have said, "After all the excuses and stories and perspectives, the reason my wife left me is simple: I did not love her well enough."

Family and friends have taken exception to me saying this about myself, which gives me pause, which gives me this opportunity to elaborate.

I loved my wife with all of my heart. I think this tale of mine partly illustrates what I was willing to do for her and for our family, but the end of the story, the result, is the same. I did not love her "well enough."

I think there is a person out there who could have loved her better, given her what she needed, recognized that what she said she wanted and what she really needed are two different things; he would have been more patient, just a few minutes longer, listened better, was not as insecure as myself, was more focused on her and not the children, was stronger than me in standing up to her demands.

I believe that there is a captain out there who could have met my wife's needs and managed the situation better than myself, but that person was not me. I loved my wife dearly, just not well enough to fulfill her needs. I hope there is a person for her. I pray she will find him.

Pop and Zen

My Uncle Jim, my mother's brother, was a trick rider. He was small and agile, a little crazy and very brave. He was also fearless. The combination of bravery and fearlessness was the recipe for a trick rider.

The average horse stands about 6' at the withers (where the shoulder meets the neck). Add three feet for the torso of the man riding plus the distance a horse leaves the ground at a gallop and that distance from the ground is easily ten feet.

Take two horses and two riders and set them off on a gallop (I can't even hold on to a horse for a gallop) so the horses are stride for stride and pinned close together.

That is the moment when James Dougherty would stand on the shoulders of the riders, one foot on each rider, high above the crowd, to unfurl the American Flag for a lap around the arena.

Uncle Jim was a trick rider. He was more than a one trick pony.

One day Pop was telling me about rodeos and horses and his saddles. Pop was in his early 70's at the time and I was just learning to listen. My father, for most of my life, was a man in passing. He was going to work and I was going somewhere else and we never talked until those last dozen years or so.

In reference to Uncle Jim, Pop said, "I bought him his first trick riding saddle."

Saddles cost a bunch of money today and a bunch back then.

"Why did you buy him a saddle?" I asked.

Pop was simple. Pop was more Zen that any person I have met. He didn't read Lao Tzu (please read the Tao de Ching) nor anything by D.T. Suzuki (Zen Buddhism). Pop picked tin on the dump and rode horses, he fought and drank and fathered and worked as best he could until he couldn't work no more.

He answer marks his depth and compassion:

"Cause he didn't have none," said Pop.

The comment encapsulates Pop and his beliefs, generosity, simplicity and shite Philadelphia grammar.

They went into a shop, Uncle Jim saw the saddle and his friend bought it for him, "Cause he didn't have none."

I hope in my life to make one decision with such purity. I hope to make one comment in my life that is beyond me and my mind and rings true like Joseph Murphy's comment. I can only hope that someday I will arrive as close to mindless perfection as my father's action 50 years before and his description of that action 50 years later.

"Hail Mary, full of Grace, the Lord is with thee…"

Chapter 4: Take a Bus.

I slept more on this second walk than on the first year because the sun was more intense with not a cloud in the sky. Every few hours I lay down by the side of the road. I was still flowing through two liters of water an hour. I was miles away from a bed and the sun was beginning to set.

Estimating based on the first pilgrimage, I was still five hours out of Orotina and exhausted. I didn't think I could make it.

I gave up. I took a bus to Orotina and went to the same hotel as the previous year.

The bus ride was about 15 minutes. I felt defeated. How the hell did I walk those miles the previous year? I was lighter and more fit this year but was broken on day one.

I planned on walking the railroad track the next day. I could lie about taking the bus and no one would be the wiser. I could just not mention that I took the bus and gave up. I could come back after I finished and walk that part that I missed. There were any number of excuses I could employ.

The truth is:

I just couldn't get er' done.

"Pray for us sinners."

Chapter 5: In Abuelo's Footsteps.

The following morning I set out with prayers and confidence. I ate a hearty breakfast. The sun was already brutal at 8am.

I asked the waitress where the railroads tracks were. She pointed me three blocks down the road and I followed.

I had walked near railroad tracks as a child. These tracks in Orotina were not much different. A bed of fist sized rocks made way for 6" x 6" wood ties. Much of the stones had washed away or been stolen for better use. The railroad itself stopped running in 1995 after 85 years of use.

For the first mile, houses lined either side of the rails, some looked like summer fincas (country vacation farms that produce nothing) and others were squat wooden structures built by folk who appropriated the land. Either side of the tracks provided an intermittent rocky dirt path that was used by motorbikes and travelling pilgrims.

Under an unforgiving sun, random dogs from the random shacks, barked, ran at me or ignored me because of the heat. There is no shade on those tracks and I tried to find the best walking pattern.

Walking on the ties required more concentration that I was willing to give because the ties required uneven steps and that rhythm didn't make for a pleasant walk.

Walking along the path was little better, the stones did not provide any surface that was consistent. With every step my feet would slide on the stones, just a little. Multiply that little slide by a thousand steps and the skin on your feet will wear away, at least with the shoes I had on.

I hadn't yet arrived at actual pain from the stones by after the first hour I knew this railroad walking was going to be more challenging than the road.

I had brought two liters of water and had drunk almost the entire stock during the first hour. I needed to conserve water.

The railroad runs along near the top of the mountain range from the sea to the central valley. I had moved out of the populated area and was now in upper jungle mountain territory. There were no 7-Elevens here.

How was I going to get water?

I looked at my watch. The time was 11am. I had just taken my last sip of water. I thought, "The clock on my life starts ticking now. I am starting to die, if I don't find water in three hours I will start to become weak and delirious."

Ya' can't walk for long in 95 degree heat under blazing sun without any water. If I didn't find water in the next hour, I would have to turn back to Orotina. People die from foolish adventures all the time. Costa Rica is wild and dangerous.

I remembered reading about the Head of the Park guards in the Osa Peninsula in southern in CR. He had been a guard in that park for 15 years or so, then one day he went out for a walk and never returned. His body was not recovered. I had a healthy respect for nature. This wasn't Fairmount Park or Central Park; this was middle of nowhere Costa Rica.

I walked, stumbled on rocks and prayed.

"Hail Mary, full of grace, the Lord is with thee..."

Chapter 6: Dying of Thirst.

It rains so much in Costa Rica, drinking water should never be a problem. I knew there had to be some stream running down from the mountain. I think it is hard to die from lack of water in a country that gets so much rain. I hoped anyway.

A couple of hundred yards ahead I saw a defunct railroad station. It was a two story concrete peaked roof building that was used less for passengers and more for transporting goods to the city.

Running from the top of the mountain was a stream of water flowing into a beautiful moss covered drinking trough, complete with the face of a sun with the water shooting out of the mouth.

I checked for snakes and other animals also looking for water and then filled up my bottle. It was no time to worry too much about Giardiasis or any other parasite that was in the water. I would worry about the diarrhea later, right now, my body needed liquid.

Cold, cold, mountain water.

I explored the train station. The windows were gone and spray paint from Costa Rican youth covered the walls. It looked like a great place for young folk to party. Remnants of parties littered the inside. Thankfully, no one was home.

I drank more and lay down. I was exhausted and the late morning sun was intense fire, not a breeze stirred, but I had some hope.

With some luck these railroad stations would be placed every few miles and with some more luck each would have a water source flowing from the mountain top.

My feet were a mess. My legs were cramped. I was on the side of a mountain and didn't know squat about the lay of the land. I thought of my children. I thought about where they were. We had been separated for so long. I had some hope that the Restraining Order would end, the Family Visitation sentence would come down from the Judge-gods and that my children and I would connect and live out some sort of normal life where we could read and learn and play together.

*In August 2012, Dan Knight and Soledad were coming up on a two year anniversary. She told Dan Knight that I was holding up the Divorce but that it would be final by the end of the year. He continued to give her money and visit. I continued to give her what felt like ransom.

Chapter 7: Rail Epiphany.

With the water problem solved for the moment, I continued walking but every step was pain. Every step the rocks slid just a little and that friction rubbed me raw. I lay down in the shade by the side of the tracks.

I didn't think I could walk for three more days on the unforgiving rocks. I looked at the perfection of the rails. The white sunlight glared off the smooth metal. The three inch width of rail was the only smooth surface in sight, fading off into perfection around the bend.

I thought, "If I could walk on that rail, I could walk to San Jose."

Tight rope walkers could do it. A gymnast could walk on the line. I thought of my analogy of a good Captain during a storm. For the best captain, the storm requires attention to detail and will pass, for a poor captain, all the attention to detail will not compensate for expertise.

Was I an expert walking on a rail? Not yet, but with a little help I would be after another three hours.

"Hail Mary..."

Chapter 8: Walking the Rail.

I do not discount the possibility that heat exhaustion was affecting my thought process. It was hot. The sun was a bitch.

In a flashing moment of clarity, the Virgin visited me for the first time on this trip. She spoke a voiceless message in my mind and the switches began to click into place. I began to look for a long stick that was thin, not too heavy and not too rotted or covered in anything that could harm me.

I first found a stick to look for sticks. I mentioned earlier in this book that 80% of snake bites are from the elbow down and the knee down. Start plodding through undisturbed high grass and piles of broken trees and the snakes and bees will kill you pretty quick in a swollen-up, lack-of-breathe way.

A scorpion will only numb-up the tongue, but a bunch of scorpion bites from shaking a nest and that too will expire the clock that ticks away the seconds of our lives.

I looked gingerly and thought of the French recluse who told me how he walked in the jungle at night. He always said, "con permiso" (with permission), to show his respect for the jungle.

I "con permiso-ed" myself a nice skinny six foot branch. I stripped off the excess sticks and found another less reliable stick and started on my way, walking the rail.

One foot in front of the other, knees slightly bent, eyes on the horizon with the two sticks providing just enough resistance to maintain my balance.

I walked the rail.

Dear Lord, keep me humble. I felt like a million dollars from the accomplishment of moving. I could walk at a good clip. I was speed walking to the little Black Virgin. I expected to see her in a few days.

The sun glared rail marked my singular path, long sticks provided just enough counter balance. I stopped at another defunct train station, much like the other, except with less parts missing, this station had a neighbor, an older woman sitting on the front porch of her small timber house that smelled of wood smoke.

On the other side of the tracks, a gulley carved by noisy water, rushed down into a pool 15 meters below. I concentrated on not dying and slowly made my way down the mossy wet slope, saying my prayers.

My concentration was rewarded with cool water. I wondered if the old lady wondered if I had made it down here ok.

I climbed back up to the train station and sat under the shade of the platform roof. The older lady, she must have been about 65 if she was a day, was thin like the rail and hard as a coffin nail, but unlike most woman of an age, she was a woman who would never cut her hair, which hung white, long and straight like her limbs.

She came over to the platform smiling and told me she walked on the rails using sticks to get to the next small town to buy what little she bought, just coffee, rice and sugar. She blessed my journey.

I took to heel; though felt I had tamed the horse. I walked on auto pilot, interrupted by brief balance adjustments every few seconds that with practice, stretched into whole minutes.

I thought about why I was walking. I was already suffering emotionally. Why was I making myself suffer more?

I already did this…

What good was walking on a train track on the side of a mountain really doing for my children?

I slowed my pace and the Little Black Virgin midwifed a second epiphany out of me.

She said, "Deje a sufrir."

And yes, the message was in Spanish. Most simply translated as, "Stop Suffering."

I think of it in English as, "Leave your suffering behind."

I quit the Pilgrimage and with it, self-induced suffering.

I decided to return to my bed, air conditioning and a pizza.

I had to walk for another hour or so to get to the next break-in-the-tracks town that has a dirt road and an entrance ramp to get onto the new highway. There, I got a ride to the bus stop and then a bus back to my apartment in Jaco.

I was self-flagellating. That needed to stop. I wasn't proving anything by walking or suffering. I needed a positive form of expression. I needed to write down those memories of my children.

I think that someday, maybe my children and I will finish that pilgrimage together. I can tell them the stories of Abuelo and Pop, and we can feel the Zen of walking a rail.

Chapter 9: Bet on the Home Team.

The Restraining Order expired like a silent fart on September 7, 2012.

That Family Court Judge could now give his ruling. I expected favorable. I thought my wife's no-show was a sign of disrespect. I thought the no-show after the hundreds of hours invested by the courts revealed a nature that was in contempt of the courts.

The judge was still waiting for the Psychologist report. The end of the Restraining Order coinciding with the Family Court decision was logical only in my mind. I alone invented that logic. The thought that a natural course of events would take place gave me hope for the interim months, but those final moments where hope comes to fruition, only noiseless gas exhaled.

No noise from either the Judge or the Psychologist, just the stink of recurring disappointment lingered in the air.

In a war of attrition always bet on the home team. With few historical exceptions the indigenous population has ruled the day. I was still bedfellows with Stephen Covey in my unconditional giving but I probably should have listed more towards, "The Art of War," before I made any moves. Even Machiavelli's, "The Prince," would have highlighted the errors in the fool's mission I was on. I was a foreign invader sieging with an army of one.

I had been in the country for a year and 2 months and had jumped through all the fiery hoops and landed on my feet. I was still not permitted to see or speak with my children. They were so close and yet they were forever away.

Each day that passed, I missed another moment in their lives. The moments I have chronicled here, are what I have left. At the time, I was concerned about losing time and moments and memories.

There is no recompense for lost time.

It was time for justice, but justice in Costa Rica is a late arriving lover.

Federal Maxim in the U.S. Justice System:

Justice delayed is justice denied.

I feel ya'.

You feel me?

Chapter 10: October 2012.

Never get involved in a two front war. Two front wars knocked out Napoleon and Hitler.

I was engaged in a three front battle:

1. Domestic Violence Court: Restraining order ended. Nothing pending but always a risk that my wife would ask to re-instate.

2. Family Court: Waiting for the Psychologist report since April. Judge will decide on Visitation Schedule after he receives the Psych Report.

3. Child Support: I was paying $800 without a court mandate when I arrived. Court increased to $900 in March 2012. My wife was now requesting an increase in payment. She requested $1,800 (This was an impossible number for me. Keep in mind that in PA the lawyer said it would be $1,000 at most).

How do you think I faired thus far?

Three days, three weeks, three months…I wait.

"Hail Mary, full of grace…"

Chapter 11: Child Support.

For the third time, the police showed-up at my condo. A lone messenger came on his motorbike in the late afternoon. I had developed a good relationship with the police. The first time they showed-up at my apartment I cried. I showed them my paid receipts and they drove away.

After the second time they showed-up, I sent a letter to the Captain commending his Sergeant and officers for being so polite. It was a "thanks for not tasering me" letter. I really appreciated the professionalism. I didn't cry that time.

For this third visit, I was paid-up with child support. I showed the Police Officer my recent monthly payment receipt and made a photocopy for him to take with him.

We said, "Good-bye," like he was the Fed Ex guy with a sidearm, delivering a package.

I lived in constant expectation that the police would arrive for me at any minute. I lived the psychology of the criminal. The mentality of the criminal awaiting arrest is like coffee and cigarettes, you might not start out liking them, but after time and use, by way of attrition, ya' get used to em'.

The trick was feeling like I wasn't guilty of any crimes but yet being under the threat of incarceration. As an innocent, I went to the police station the next day to get a copy of the Order of Capture from the previous night. I wanted to know why the police had come to arrest me.

Jaco had just built a new police station. They moved from their cramped quarters in front of the beach to an airy new clean building along the Coastal Road.

I drove over in the afternoon, still in my school clothes; I asked the young lady at reception if I could see the Order of Capture from the previous night.

Her eyes lit up when she heard my name. "Oh, one minute. Jose, where is that Capture Order from last night against Murphy?"

She and two other young coppers working the desk went about trying to find the document.

I sat and watched the comedy play out: "Hhhmmmm, where do we put those Order of Capture Warrants....could be just about anywhere....Give us a few minutes."

After a full ten minutes the Order of Capture warrant made its way to the desk. I read the warrant and showed the clerk my receipt from the current month's payment. In fact, I had brought my file with me of every monthly payment made from the previous year.

She pointed out that the Pension had increased. I was never notified. Instead of paying $900 a month, I was now ordered to pay $1,600 a month.

"Do you have $700 with you?"

I thought, "Oh sure, I always carry my entire monthly salary from the school with me..." but said, "No, but I can go to the ATM machine and come back".

"No" she said, "You can't leave."

I put my wrists together and offered for her to put handcuffs on me. She smiled and said, "No, no, no...it is not like that." They didn't need to cuff me but yet I couldn't leave either.

She asked if someone could bring me the money. I was in custody until I produced $700. That much was certain.

One of the Lieutenants was my neighbor. I asked him if he could lend me an escort to take me to the ATM machine. He told me they were changing shifts and the police trucks (they use Toyota Hilux) were out at the moment.

I told him I had my car, so he lent me an overweight rookie flunky to join me for a ride to the ATM. I drove.

I had the money. I paid the money. But what about next month and then December when the amount doubles? What then?

Chapter 12: A Decision She Can Appeal?

The day came in late October 2012, when the Psychologist report was filed and the Family Court Judge arrived at a decision.

I was given supervised visits; two Sunday's a month, in the house of my father-in-law.

I was crushed by the decision for many reasons.

My father-in-law was the guy who thought I had magic cancer powder. How long would it take before I was reported for poor behavior? How many visits would I get in before he reported that the children were afraid of me?

I would have to video tape every minute of every visit to have a record. The situation was miserable but at least I had gained something. Great, just let me see my children.

My attorney gave me the news and then she dropped the next two bombshells on me and my life hasn't been the same since. What anemic hope I had went into liver failure and died that day.

I was no longer on a three day, three week, three months' timetable. The timetable had been extended.

First, my wife had to be notified by hand. Successfully notifying my wife at her house happened only once in this process. Weeks and weeks had passed trying to notify her of anything. (Remember me sitting with Christmas presents? Couldn't get her notified then.)

I could expect that the process of notifying my wife would take 6 weeks.

Secondly, my wife could *appeal* the decision.

I lost it. I dropped the phone. I screamed "Motherfucker" once, at the top of my lungs. I screamed, "No, no, no, you have got to be kidding me."

My wife didn't even appear at the first hearing. How can she appeal? How can she continue to manipulate this system?

What did an appeal mean?

We were in October. Six weeks to notify my wife if my children and I were lucky, it would then take six more months for the Appeals judge to read the case and make a decision.

During which time I would neither be allowed to see or speak with my children. If at any time I made an attempt to see or speak with my children, my wife always had the option of calling the Domestic Violence courts…"he called, he was angry, I was scared…" and the DV court will take at least another six months off the top.

I had been in the country for a year and four months and this process could easily take another 6-8 months.

Note: In February 2013, a full 3 months after the decision, I received a notice that my wife had not yet been notified of the decision. The court warned her that she must give a valid address to be notified.

Three months after the decision and I was still supposed to waiting around to see my children, content that the system was moving forward.

It is a legal system without teeth that occasionally gummed the manipulators.

I was nearing an alternative junction in the road. My expectation of a fair ball game ended.

Chapter 13: Aguinaldo.

Aguinaldo is a double payment of salary in the month of December for all Costa Rican employees. Aguinaldo gives the whole country cash to spend at Christmas. Aguinaldo is a bonus mandated by law. Cool.

I learned that Child Support has an Aguinaldo but my job as a "consultant" at the school did not.

The numbers: $1,600 to be paid both on the 1st and 15th of December then $1,600 to be paid on the first of January. Within one month I would be required to pay $4,800.

There also exists a School Bonus in January which runs about $600, then February 1 comes around the corner.

From December 1 until February 1: I would need $7,000.

I would earn about half of that amount. I had a little over three grand in the bank. I still had to eat, pay rent, pay lawyers, pay the credit card bills my wife left in my name and drive to San Jose.

I considered my options: jail, borrow more money, run.

Chapter 14: Jail.

If I were a day late (and I never was) with my Child Support Payment, the police would arrive a few days later.

If I did not have sufficient funds, I would be taken into custody and placed in a small room with a wooden bunk. I would need to feed myself, so I would order pizzas from my friends at Pizza Palma.

At the Jaco station, I could probably stay in custody for three days, but after that time I would be transferred to the real prison in Puntarenas.

Most likely, I could make a deal with the coppers in Jaco to stay a few days longer in their cell before being moved to General Population (GP) at Puntarenas which lies about 30 minutes north of Jaco. I later learned that I would not be in GP at Puntarenas but jail is jail any way you look at it.

Statistically speaking, more so than on the outside, there was an increased chance that within the first 48 hours I would either kill someone or be killed.

A higher possibility would be some sort of physical confrontation: fists and prison shanks and blood. (I just like the word shank and use it every opportunity I can. "I'll have the shank." I need to learn the word for "shank" in Spanish – put that on the list.)

I had played out this scenario in high school on my first day transferring to the Catholic High School from a Private Prep School. The attacker in Costa Rica would be a little guy with a big man complex, just like in high school.

I was not keen on the "Go to Prison" scenario. I also know that I wasn't going to find any child support money in there. That much was certain.

Chapter 15: Borrow the Money.

I could borrow the money from my parents and try to hang on for the next year. Live meager, sell the car, move to a dangerous dirty neighborhood and rent a cheap apartment.

During this hard living phase, I would still be removed from the lives of my children.

As a long term solution borrowing money and hoping to make at least $3,000 a month in Costa Rica or online looked to be a path of high struggle and low return on investment with the distinct possibility of going to jail for lack of funding on any given month.

I would still be a father to fatherless children. No contact. No love.

Chapter 16: Running Option.

To be fair, running had always been an option. Would I need to exercise that option? What tension would add to the calculus that would unbalance the Cost/Benefit Analysis? What did the perfect storm like? How would I get out?

Like so many decisions in life, this would come down to time and money.

Time: Towards the end of October, I had been almost 18 months in country and involved in the court system with the goal of seeing my children. I was looking at another year without communication. Domestic Violence standards being what they are, at any time during the process my wife could use the system to her advantage and add more separation time.

Money: I had enough to leave the country now. In two months I would have less than zero. Then how would I leave the country? There was a good chance I was going to jail. I could not sustain that amount of Child Support and having the amount of Child Support reduced had already been rejected.

How would I get out?

The northern border with Nicaragua is a sieve. I could sell the car or have a driver leave me three miles before the border. I would run diagonal to the San Juan River which separates the countries. I would either swim or look for a friendly local with a launch. I would then run the hypotenuse to the road at a 3 mile mark where my driver would retrieve me on the Nicaraguan side.

That scenario would be an 8-10 mile cross country run through rough territory (read snakes) plus a swim (factor in crocodiles). The heat would be heavy during the day and nighttime would be way too scary for me, so earliest in the morning would be best.

Nothing like a run in the park.

The southern border of Costa Rica and Panama is also a sieve. I Googled "how to cross the border illegally in Costa Rica" and got 10,000,000 hits.

There is a village in the center of the country along the border called Rio Serreno. There were several stories on the net about people who drove across the border and didn't know they had changed countries until they saw different color taxis (CR are red; Panama are yellow).

Rio Serreno here I come.

I figured I would enter Panama, get myself an Entrance stamp and be on my merry way.

Good bye Costa Rican Justice System. Adios.

Before I made any decision, I first wanted to negotiate with my Soledad.

"Hail Mary, full of grace..."

Chapter 17: Negotiate.

I sent my wife an email stating that I couldn't pay $1,600. I also told her that I had no intention of going to jail.

I offered her $1,000 a month and I wanted every other weekend visits and three times during the week with unlimited phone calls (this is exactly the plan she proposed when I asked her the worst case scenario two years before when we lived in the U.S.).

Why would she accept this? Well, she wouldn't, the courts said $1,600 a month and supervised visits with no phone calls.

I told my wife I would leave the country if she was not willing to negotiate on the visits and cash.

She wrote me back saying that, "You can't leave the country." She had the weight of the police behind her; she had the justice system behind her. We had not negotiated since I entered Costa Rica. She had been in the driver's seat and my destination was jail.

I wasn't bluffing but she wasn't negotiating.

I responded and said, "You would rather take nothing than $1,000?"

Her response: You can't leave.

Watch me.

*I still didn't know Dan Knight was giving Soledad money, he told her to forget money. He offered to give her money she thought I owed her, just to close the chapter and move on with their lives. She refused.

Chapter 18: Brute Irish Tactics.

My lawyer made one final appeal to the Child Support Courts. My request for reducing the payment was denied. The judge stated that I should have been, "saving up" for the Aguinaldo.

I made my decision to leave Costa Rica. I gave-up on any justice from the courts. I had tried for 18 months with not a ray of sunshine. Total failure, while lots of money went into the pockets of lawyers; lost money that did nothing to benefit my children.

And the children?

I wasn't abandoning Sean, Ted and Elizabeth. I was changing negotiating tactics. I shifted into Brute Irish tactics. "I can't see the kids?" "Then no money for you." I figured I would try this tactic for the same amount of time that I spent wearing the white hat following the Justice System of Costa Rica.

I believe that the best option of seeing my children is placing financial pressure on my wife. I believe that if I had a meeting with my children and I laid out our situation, that Ted and Sean would agree with my decision. Unfortunately, I don't know Elizabeth and she doesn't know me, so I couldn't really speak to her opinion.

We may take our lumps in the short run; however, I was looking at the long term.

I abandoned righteousness and my role as a victim.

I had felt like a criminal in Costa Rica for 18 months, now I would be one. From teacher and husband, to father on the run: refuse payment of child support, elude police and illegally cross the border and come up for air in a friendly country and accept a new identity: deadbeat dad.

I kept praying, day and night…

Part VI

Escape from Costa Rica

October 2012 – May 2015

Chapter 1: Iris.

In late October 2012, on a Friday morning, I found myself in Largato, the local hardware store in Jaco Beach. I needed to buy paint for our school play. The scenery was done by our in-house professional thespian. My job was to manage the funds, provide support and go buy the paint.

I saw her from 60 feet. She was lithe and loaded with energy and confidence. I made my way to the paint section where she was talking with a salesman. She looked like she was going to ask him at least dozen questions with multiple scenarios. She had her sun glasses slid down her nose, so when she looked at me as I passed, I knew I had her attention.

She wore silky black drawstring wide bottom pants and a tight fitting tank-top. She swished around the aisles. I imagined she was the Italian wife of a lucky man, preparing to re-model the kitchen for lack of anything better to do.

I wanted to meet her just the same.

She swished past me, her flips flops slapping the concrete floor, beating the rhythm for the rise and fall of her backside. She was my age, around 40; I had little doubt that she had already garnered a rich husband who was probably just an all-around great guy. She looked like she deserved nothing less.

That guy found the dream woman. I wanted to find the dream woman. I decided that I could be that guy if I just interviewed enough woman and continued to live the noble life of father, educator, communicator, emotionally aware with good energy, low drama, high honesty, heavy listening, super fit, funny, borderline successful (with good potential), intelligent, humble, not easily riled, vulnerable, considerate, clean and organized living type of beach guy.

Outweighing all else was my baggage.

I realized that I had had my shot at love and a family. I was now in the damaged goods department, a dented can of beans but still looking pretty good next to the crushed box of saltines. I wasn't "out of code," just yet.

I will be that guy. I will find that woman and she will love me as much as I love her. It is easy to fall in love and be all crazy over a person (especially this woman) and think you want to be with them forever; finding the person that feels the SAME way about you is a whole 'nother ball game.

I would be happy with "Hello," and see if I could get a smile out of her. That would be enough.

The computer system was down so check-out was in a holding pattern. I had no time to hold pattern, so I left and chalked-up not meeting her to the fates. After I dropped my car off at the mechanic, I folded myself into his loaner Le Car to return to Largato to buy the paint.

She was still there, waiting for the system to return. This woman really wanted that paint.

I stepped into line behind her and she turned to me.

"What are we going to paint today?" I asked.

Just then, the cashier announces to Iris, "Ya, estamos listos," "Now, we are ready."

"Wait, wait" I said to the cashier, acting nervous and laughing, "I am just getting started here." Humor, confidence and vulnerability broke the ice.

"My name is John Murphy. What's your name?"

"Iris."

"It is a pleasure to meet you Iris."

She placed her tin of white paint on the counter.

The clock was ticking and she was stepping out the door in less than two minutes.

I asked for her telephone number but she was visiting and didn't have one. She said she could give me her email. I asked the cashier for her pen. She was now ringing up my items but my purchase was clearly secondary to getting this woman's contact information.

She wrote with the pen on a bumpy surface so the writing was hard to make out. The pen was also giving out on ink and faded towards the end.

Got it.

We exchanged goodbyes and I told her I would send her an email.

Chapter 2: Persistence.

I couldn't read the email address for a good god darn. Seven possible email addresses failed me but the eighth was lucky.

On our first date we went for a walk on Hermosa Beach to look at drift wood. We did not kiss.

Iris came to dinner the next night. We moved-in together two days later and have been together about 22 hours a day ever since.

She paints. I write.

Alright.

Chapter 3: The Present.

I learned to live in the present. Iris is one month older than I am. She has a 24 year old son. She was exactly the woman I was looking for. I had dated women in their twenties and thirties. Those women wanted babies and a family. I had a family. I had babies. There was no future for me with a woman who wanted children.

We talked and talked and enjoyed the silence between the words. She too, lives in the present.

I spoke about my plans to pack-up and move to Panama and the circumstances of the law. I held nothing back. I had no interest in conning anyone to take this trip with me. In fact, I imagined the journey being easier alone.

I continued to try and negotiate with my wife. I sent an email to her mother and her sister telling them of my plans to leave. I posed the situation to her family like this:

Imagine your son moved to another country to be with his children.

He had spent 18 months trying to regain contact without success.

He had another year of appeals waiting, with no child contact.

He was going to prison for lack of funds.

What advice would you give your son?

Neither my wife nor her family responded to my scenario or the offer of $1,000 a month plus visits.

As a negotiating tactic, not responding made sense. I can appreciate that. Why negotiate on "ifs?" "If" I leave the country and "if" I can escape.

Put up or shut up is the playground rule.

Fair 'nough.

We can have this same conversation when I am in Panama.

My hand was forced. Between the choices of going to prison or leaving the country, I chose a life of travel.

And that has made all the difference.

Chapter 4: Physical Emotional Pain.

During this time of leaving Jaco, I experienced debilitating back pain. I subscribe to the notion that physical ailments are emotional ailments manifesting themselves in the body.

My back pain was the physical manifestation of all the emotional pain of the last two years. I realized at the time that there are only three positions in this life. You are either sitting, standing or lying down.

I could do any one of these positions for no more than 5 minutes at a time. After 5 minutes my back would tighten. The pain was blinding. Sometimes it hurt so much it made me laugh. How could sneezing cause so much pain? Sleeping was fits of quiet mixed with dull pain.

I stretched and stretched and gave self-massages. I found the exact spot where the pain was born and kneaded the muscles like dough.

I mended myself slowly at Playa Coyote, visiting with my longtime friends Manuel, Caroline and their daughter Ana. I couldn't dive or surf because of the pain. Iris and I spent quiet days playing with Ana and talking with Caroline and Manuel.

PreToma is the nonprofit environmental group for whom Manuel and Caroline work. Each Christmas, friends of PreToma in San Jose collect clothes for the families of fisherman.

We went to the one of the fishing villages where the families lined up to receive their Christmas gifts. Manuel and Caroline are touching lives, making an impact on the environment both with the fishies and turtles in the sea and the people who live off of those resources on land.

I wanted my children with me. They could learn from this experience. Manuel and Caroline are people I admire, they are people that my children deserve to have in their lives. Someday they will. I reassured myself that the universe was unfolding, that my children will someday experience the goodness of the people I hold dear to my heart.

Always, in the back of my mind were two questions:

What are my children doing now?

Why can't they be here with me now?

Now, there is only one question:

What are my children doing now?

I have accepted what the universe has given, and what the universe has taken away.

"Hail Mary full of grace, the Lord is with thee…"

Chapter 5: Up and Up to Rio Serreno.

We left Manuel, Caroline and Ana, in the early morning hours, with hugs and farewells. It was never a goodbye. We would meet again in this life.

Iris and I drove down the Pacific Coast of Costa Rica for 7 hours to arrive at Ciudad Nelly by mid-afternoon. We stopped for coffee and pastries at a stale looking bakery where we decided to try for Rio Serreno this very night. Why wait?

As the road moved into the interior of the country, the lowland beach landscape drifted out of focus. The new landscape was wet mountain. We climbed for forty five minutes up the mountain. We entered the clouds and then drifted through the high plateaus. I expected to see Highlander Scots in tartan, with bone handled knives tucked neatly into their socks, like little kids without pockets.

We stopped at an overlook to give the car a needed rest. This mountain was not for the faint of car. After an hour of climbing we plateaued again and cruised into a small village comprised of a few hundred souls, a mechanic, grocery store, a tiny school and a soccer pitch.

I asked two old boys sitting roadside, "Which way to Rio Serreno?" They pointed to the right. We continued to rise with the mountain. This was the highest climb in a car I had ever made. I couldn't imagine the mountain rising higher. I am surprised to find that the elevation is only passing over 4,000 feet because we climbed for over an hour from sea level.

The paved road ended and a rocky gravelly road continued to the left. The road was less a road and more a moon crater experience. The sun had set an hour before and the last glimpses of light faded.

There were no houses or shops, just bumpy road. We had been travelling a full 12 hours, we were looking for an illegal border crossing and it was dark. A car passing in the opposite direction gave us hope. Someone was coming from somewhere. We decided to continue for another 15 minutes and if we found nothing we would return down the mountain to the first place that would rent us a place to sleep.

The road straightened out and there was more traffic and lights up ahead. To the left, I saw the small blue and white Costa Rican Police Station. These were the exact fellows we were looking to avoid. A bus was parked in the middle of the road (presumably to allow passengers to have their passports checked by the Immigration Police). I passed to the right of the bus, bore right and suddenly the road became blacktopped and separated by double yellow lines.

The taxis changed color and we were in a shopping district with bars and restaurants and sundry stores selling everything from flat screens and refrigerators to dollar store junk. Mannequins from clothing stores saluted Iris and me.

We were in Panama. We made it. Costa Rican Justice was an idea in the past. I am free.

Or was I?

Chapter 6: High Mountain Freedom.

We were on top of the mountain. I felt high up in the Adirondacks or deep in the Smokies. This mountain was not unlike the Appalachians in Pennsylvania. The environment of crisp air, the threat of cold and the dense 100 year old pines sticking out of the mountain like random birthday candles made me feel at home.

Home is not always a safe feeling. Night had set, fog was grazing, and there were no streetlamps on this backwoods mountain road in Panama. The cutbacks were dizzying. After more than 12 hours on the road, I knew that extra precaution was needed. Accidents and arguments (from lack of energy) happen when people are tired.

We coasted down in second gear, free of heavy braking but no less on edge. Panama has excellent roads. The blacktop was crisp and new with professional double yellow lines that seemed like a luxury compared to the battle scarred, unlined roadways in Costa Rica.

We drifted down the mountain, thinking that I was free of the laws of Costa Rica. Tomorrow we would head directly to Panama City where Iris' son lives. We would look for a home along the coastline, a beach town, preferably with some waves and enough people for a small town feel. We also needed reliable internet service. I could run my on-line classes from anywhere.

In fact, I was still teaching Spanish to one class of Gifted 2nd to 5th graders from Pennsylvania. The students and I had discussed where I was in Central America (one of the students had been to Costa Rica) and where I was going. We did a quick project on the history of the Panama Canal.

I was also writing a Proposal for Services for the New York City Department of Education. My business is education. I needed to keep the office open. My office was anywhere with Wi-Fi. I could get on-line and teach a class and use my Magicjack to return phone calls to the United States. Magicjack is voice over the internet for

$40 of unlimited calling per year, to the U.S., from anywhere in the world.

Reliable internet access was essential to our next home.

We stayed the night at the base of the Volcano Baru. At "Il Forno," we ate pizza made by an Italian chef and served by his Columbian wife. We drank Coca Cola and listened to Madame Butterfly.

With no exit stamps or entrance stamps, we were both illegal, driving an illegal car, filled with our worldly possessions.

If you live in the present it was just another car ride and a pizza for dinner.

I chose to live in the present. I had lingered for two years in the past and the savagery of my emotions was killing me in a long and sappy one act tragedy.

I never doubted my move to leave Costa Rica.

Chapter 7: Stereotype Predictions Come True.

I am an open minded guy. I consider myself a citizen of the world. I would categorize my parents as more conservative. Anyone who was from somewhere else but the USA was second best and anyone from a third world country was less than third best.

My parents' opinion that I was marrying a Costa Rican was one of subtle dismay. "Are you sure you want to marry someone from another country?"

My parents' were sure they had raised a witless son when I told them I was allowing Soledad to leave the country with the children. "You won't have any rights down there... They will screw you because you're a gringo... She will take those kids away... You'll get put in jail...

All of those stereotypical opinions came to pass. All of 'em.

They were right.

But that is the short term consequence. If my wife thought our best chance of reconciliation was her going to Costa Rica first while I continued to work in the U.S., then I would give it to her.

I wanted to live in Costa Rica anyhow, so why not?

I lived by my principles and rolled the fuckin' dice.

And because of that, Iris and I have finally found each other. We have been running towards one another for centuries.

I accept the perfection of the universe.

Chapter 8: Stuck in No Man's Land.

In the morning, we rose early and drove three hours until we arrived in the middle of the country and we were real surprised to find an Immigration Checkpoint so far from the border. Since there is only one highway through Panama it is a good place to put a control area. I know that now. I didn't know it then as we braked and waited for the young, armed, vested Immigration Official.

We explained that I was a teacher with a few weeks off for break and that we were travelling in Panama. Our passports had been stolen the night before and we were on our way to the Embassy in Panama City to replace the documents.

He asked us to pull to the shoulder where we waited in the shade while he made phone calls to people who knew more than him.

When he returned to the car his face was grim. He told us to turn around and go back to Antonio, the largest city on this side of the Immigration Control, and go to U.S. Consular services.

We went through the range of excuses…we were late, family was waiting in Panama City and Antonio was three hours in the opposite direction and nothing worked.

Turn around.

Maybe this escape thing wasn't so easy. We were stuck in no man's land between the official border crossing in Paso Canoas and the Immigration Check-point in the center of the country. Our world had grown smaller.

Before we left on this trip I consulted with my contact at the U.S. Embassy in Costa Rica. I had been consulting with an official at the U.S. Embassy since I first arrived in Costa Rica. The official had made inquiries into my case. My contact had called the Costa Rican Courts several times to inquire as to the case but the Embassy does not get officially involved in the Costa Rican Court Process. My lawyer and the Consular official told me that the Costa Rican government is very touchy about U.S. involvement in their system.

I consulted my contact at U.S. Consular Services in Costa Rica and posed my hypothetical scenario:

If a person escaped Costa Rica, entered Nicaragua or Panama illegally and reported their passport stolen at the U.S. Embassy, what would happen? Would the U.S. check the Entrance Stamp or simply issue a new passport.

I was told that if "a person" could make it across *and* get to the Embassy that there would not be an issue of Entrance and Exit stamps.

OK. We turned around and went back to Antonio to find the U.S. Consulate.

Problem is, there is no U.S. Consulate in Antonio.

On the fly, we made our decision to go to the border at Paso Canoas and find out more about getting the Entrance Stamp on my passport. We also had a car which needed some type of clearance.

One thing for sure is that we weren't getting past that checkpoint in the middle of Panama.

I was heading back into the lion's den.

Chapter 9: Bribe Him.

We thought we could enter Paso Canoas from the Panamanian side and Iris could get her Exit Stamp and we could see what the movement was with the stamps. If I could just get the Entrance Stamp from Panama and not the Exit Stamp from Costa Rica, then I would be free.

The Panamanians at the Paso Canoas border have things locked down. The border area is free and easy but there is a check point several miles from the border. We had no choice but to pass. I couldn't pull a U-turn and bolt out of there, nor did I want to live the rest of my days in that strip of Panama. We spoke with the guard and he let us pass to get our stamps.

Our world got even smaller: we were stuck in No-Man's land on the Panamanian side of the border. I couldn't return to Costa Rica without being arrested, and I couldn't go back through that last check point without an Exit Stamp from Costa Rica and an Entrance Stamp from Panama.

Bribery seemed my only recourse. I can do that.

At every border in the world there are people making money doing something illegal. I needed to find the right people who would not rip me off in the process and who had the connections to get my passport stamped illegally with a Costa Rican Exit stamp.

How much would that cost and who is the guy who can make it happen?

We pulled up to the filthy area surrounding the Immigration offices of Panama. Buses and trucks passing through make walking a hazard in the toxic air. In any given bureaucracy, legal or otherwise, there are three levels of people that help solve problems.

I was looking to get involved in the, "Bribe Immigration Officials" market. The first level is the mid-50's toothless alcoholic/drug addict who self-medicates and helps park the cars. He will secure a safe spot and watch your car for a few dollars. He approached my car and guided me into the spot along the street.

When he approached me to ask what I needed, I knew I had encountered the first level of criminal who would help me with my plan.

"I need a fake stamp on a U.S. Passport to Exit Costa Rica."

Obviously, this task was one above his pay grade. He was capable of three responsibilities: "helping" me park the car, watching the car and finding me the next criminal in the food chain.

He ran off in hopes of a good tip. He came back five minutes later with a young 20ish boy who wore new sneakers, Levis, a Quicksilver t-shirt and carried an IPhone for business purposes. I tipped out the old boy with $5 and he was happy with the ROI.

Young-bull spoke some English and was the next level of hustler. I told him what we needed and he said to wait in front of customs until he returned. He was young and cocky and liked the role of problem solver. He is most likely still walking No Man's Land in his Nike's, looking to assist foreigners with what they need: hookers, drugs, guided help through the Immigration Process or just basic tourist info. He felt he was the man.

I hoped he was the man.

He wasn't.

He couldn't get that type of stamp but he had an uncle who might help.

Enter level three of the Criminal Hierarchy. Young-bull told us to wait for his uncle at the Black Soup Restaurant.

After 30 minutes of waiting and watching soccer on the grease stained TV screen, the uncle arrived. He sat and we ordered coffee. As the highest level of criminal at the border, he no longer walked No Man's Land and hustled the streets. He sat at home and waited for people to call him.

He was early fifties with new sneakers, a flash fake gold watch and a leather fanny pack. He was neat in appearance and looked fresh from the barber. He was slight of build and walked with the air of a man who solves problems.

I explained my situation. I needed an exit stamp. I was buried with child support. There was nothing criminal. He was not allowing a Child Molester or a Murderer to escape. I mentioned that in case he had some conscience with his illegal activity. I imagine the price goes up based on the need. Murders probably pay more of a premium and I was looking to low ball him.

He told me that he could give me a Maritime Stamp right now for $700 but since I had a car I needed to legally cross the border with, the Maritime option was out. He could get me the stamp but it would cost $1,300. He asked for my passport and the $1,300 up front.

He looked like a serious man. I was a serious man. In any given business arrangement it all comes down to trust. A contract is just a piece of paper that someone can abide by or not. All we have is our "Word of Honor."

I told him that I would give him $400 now and the balance when I had the stamp.

I slipped the cash in my passport and sat it on the table. He casually palmed the passport and slipped it into his fanny back.

We exchanged telephone numbers. His nephew went to retrieve the car with Iris and he directed us to a cheap hotel just two blocks from the Immigration Offices. The Uncle said he would stop over in the morning after he spoke with his contact.

He told us to lay low. I am a big bald gringo and Iris is an attractive Venezuelan. We did not want any police looking at us and remembering us for any reason. Get spotted at the border for more than a day or two and the police may become suspicious.

Also, being seen talking with a bad guy puts everyone at risk. The police know the traffickers. Let's call our guy Don Juan. Don Juan had been working the border for 20 years. He had seen everything come and go and he had to keep fresh recruits coming into his system – newly appointed immigration officials.

These low level officials do the work at the window. They are the government workers you meet at any window. Not so bright, reaching for twenty years and then that pension. They are not generally people who aspire for more than the security of a government job and an occasional bribe to augment their meager income.

Things were getting hairy because now I was a criminal. Bribing an immigration official or attempting to falsify a passport sounds like a crime to me. Maybe I could get a lawyer and get out of it with bargaining and more baksheesh, but the point is, I would be spending some time incarcerated.

Put that right there at the top of my, "Things to Avoid List." I had easily avoided prison my entire life and now I was very close to the edge of that experience.

I left behind being a school teacher, a father, and a husband and entered into a new role: criminal.

Chapter 10: Vamonos.

The following day we got the call in the afternoon. Don Juan's man was working, but a supervisor from San Jose was visiting the station. If the supervisor left before 7pm, we could make the transaction today, if not, we would have to wait until the following day.

We ate Burger King and watched Netflix.

Don Juan called at 7pm and said there was no chance of completing the transaction tonight. We would wait until tomorrow.

Sit tight, lay low, wait in the shadows and watch Netflix.

The following day Don Juan called us in the morning. He told us to meet him at 11am at the Black Soup Restaurant. Don Juan liked his cloak and dagger business. "He was the pro. Listen well and do what he says," I told myself. This would all resolve itself today.

I would either be travelling in Panama with all my documents in order or I would be in prison in Costa Rica with all my documents in order, so why worry?

At 11:30am, Don Juan called us and asked us to sit in the small square that is the center of the border immigration traffic. The No Man's Zone at the square was heavily patrolled by Costa Rican police. They stood about in groups of two or three and smoked cigarettes and looked at pretty girls.

We sat on a bench and watched the goings-on for two hours. At 1:30pm, Don Juan appeared in front of a shop about 30 meters away. We made eye contact and that was all. There was a group of three police standing behind us as we causally smoked cigarettes and drank coffee, seemingly an innocuous couple lounging, people watching and waiting for something.

Don Juan passed by us amid a throng of people and said, "Follow me," without a glance in our direction.

We followed him at a distance to a large, very much empty, Chinese Restaurant that sits across the street from the Costa Rican Immigration Control Offices.

We all sat down together and ordered coffee.

He told us that we would have to wait for a phone call from his guy about when the coast was clear.

I bought an extra pack of cigarettes and slipped Iris my watch in case I ended up in the slammer.

After an hour or so, a twenty-something chubby boy approached our table and said, "Are you John Murphy?"

I am certain that our faces betrayed our surprise. Don Juan didn't know this kid. Who the hell was he and how did he know my name?

"¿Quien quiere saber?" I asked. Who wants to know?

"Nothing, Enrique sent me over to tell you that it won't be long now. I don't know anything. I just have that message."

Don Juan took the lead to dispel the fear that had crept into boy's face. He was just a messenger and didn't have any idea of the situation. Don Juan thanked the young man and we all wiped away beads of nervous sweat. A group "Whew," passed through all of us and we nervously laughed and smiled.

I realized then, that I couldn't be a criminal by profession. There would be too much stress and paranoia involved, constantly thinking, "Are they coming for me?"

I was only a few hours into my caper and already tired from the stress of thinking that several police officers were about to march across the street and beat me into cuffs and haul me away.

We eyed everyone who entered the restaurant.

There was one gringo looking fellow, he was in his mid 50's, he wore khaki fatigues and black boots. He had a lanyard hanging from his neck and I could see a Leatherman hitched to his side. Everything about him looked to be some kind of a cop. His short haircut and aviator glasses, the way he walked and stood. This guy was some kind of law enforcement.

He walked to the side of the restaurant and looked in the window of the closed photocopy shop then entered the restaurant and went to the counter to speak with the terse Chinese man, they exchanged words but he bought nothing.

He marched right up to our table and my heart was skipping beats. I felt deflated and defeated. I immediately resigned myself to some time in jail. This was a calculated risk and I would eat the results.

He kept walking right on past us. My eyes followed him until he crossed the road. Maybe he was scouting us and the exits before he came in with his boys.

Or maybe he was just a decked out gringo, both professional and scary to my guilty conscience. He mounted a BMW Touring Motorcycle with hard cased saddle bags and road dust. This soldier of fortune outfit matched his expensive touring bike. He was just a guy riding through Central American. Of course he looked like a professional badass, he was, but he wasn't coming for me.

I felt the relief as I exhaled. "No way, I never want to be a criminal," I said to Iris.

I wiped the sweat from my brow. Don Juan's phone rang.

He looked at me and said one word: "Vamanos."

Chapter 11: One Wet Finger.

We walked from the shade of the restaurant into the blazing sun and crossed the dusty street towards some form of destiny. Iris went first to one of the six windows. I stood to the side and pretended to wait for somebody, like just another traveler at Immigration except in my head, I was the Roger Moore version of James Bond.

Don Juan subtly nodded toward window number four and mouthed the word, "Cuatro." A young man exchanged a look with Don Juan and the transaction was on.

At the service window, the attendant took my passport and pretended to run the magnetic bar code under the scanner. He then gave the document a mighty stamp. Immediately, he licked his finger and smeared the ink of the serial number off the stamped page. He then took two steps out of my sight and returned with a new stamp. This was the VOID stamp. Since the first stamp was smeared he placed a Void over top of the original stamp.

Meanwhile, I hummed the tune from Mission Impossible.

He then took the original stamper and pounded the page again, this time he left the bottom half of the stamp off the page. This bottom part of the stamp has the serial number of the stamper. So I had two stamps, one had smudged serial number the other had a clear date but was also missing the serial number of the stamp.

He never looked me in the eye, he just handed back my passport and told me to have a nice day. I turned and walked back down the road towards Panama and their respective Immigration Control.

Iris and Don Juan fell in step with me. I expected a hand on my shoulder at any moment but just kept walking towards destiny.

I slipped Don Juan the remaining money I owed him; it came out to $1,300 for my freedom.

The sun was setting as I stood in front of the Panamanian Immigration window. I now needed an Entrance Stamp into Panama. The young man behind the glass found the page that held the two Costa Rican Exit Stamps. He gave the stamps the twice over, my heart fluttered, he raised his own stamper and BOOM!

I was in the clear.

Chapter 12: CR in the Geographical Past.

I legally entered into Panama in January 2013. Costa Rica was in the rearview mirror. The Justice System and jail were in the past. My wife's control over me was in the past. Negotiating with a gun at yer head makes for bad deals. For 18 months, I felt like the band leader of Johnny Fontane with Luca Brasi at my side.

My wife and I had not been negotiating for the past 18 months. In fact, we had not spoken to each other in all that time. We had never been in the same room together; there was no mediation and no communication.

Communication with my children had been cut off in April.

I don't know what vision they had of the future. I know they never heard my perspective on our family situation. My wife controls the information they received.

As father, I was making decisions that affect their future; they should have some say in the matter of Papá absconding from Costa Rica as a fugitive.

I held a family meeting, with Sean, Ted, Elizabeth and Soledad in absentia.

*I didn't know the extent to which Dan Knight had replaced me. He accepted my children as his own as much as possible. His relationship with Soledad was on the rocks. He couldn't tell if she was lying to him about the divorce. She blamed me for holding up the proceedings.

Chapter 13: Abandon the Justice System.

I was following the best route to communicate with my children by using financial pressure. If I continued to pay, my wife had no incentive to allow me to speak with the children. The courts had been put off the rails with filibuster and lies.

I settled into my roots. I put my Brute Irish tactics to the test.

I had left everything behind. At the time, I felt I was stripped of my role as a father but that wasn't the truth. I will always be a father to my children, no matter what the courts decide and what my wife believes.

I hadn't abandoned children; I had abandoned the CR Justice system.

I was resurrected as father forthright that day; paternity transcends the temporal arena of court systems and border lines.

I was marching to no one's drummer.

I hadn't left Sean, Ted and Elizabeth behind; I was closer to them now than I had been in the past 18 months of white hot struggle in a sea of salty tears.

"Pray for us sinners, now and at the hour of our death."

Chapter 14: Honor Among Thieves.

The day broke clear and we were still at the border. The car issue would take another morning of pay-offs. Don Juan met us at the Panamanian border office. His contact was working the window. I passed him $100 and the paperwork for my car.

The car itself was legal but taking it outside Costa Rica was prohibited. After five minutes of waiting in the line of cars, Don Juan passed by my window, pro offering the legally stamped documents and his hand. We shook.

There was honor among thieves.

We pulled away from the Paso Canoas Border.

Iris and I hoped we would never have to return there again.

On the 20th of January, there was a mediation meeting for our Divorce. My lawyer would be in attendance. I considered the meeting to be the final leg of the journey. I hoped my wife would recognize that I was out of her reach and that she would begin to negotiate.

Iris and I hauled ass to Panama City. Her twenty-four year old son lives there with his wife. I would apply for teaching jobs and we would scout beaches along the way. I thought Panama would offer the beach life that we wanted.

We were wrong, but we didn't know it just yet.

Chapter 15: Santa Catalina.

After a few days of visiting with Iris' son and entertaining the idea of living in Panama City, Iris and I decided we wanted the beach, so we drove for six hours to arrive at nowhere Panama. From nowhere we drove for two more hours along a winding inland road on the west coast of Panama. God Bless the Panamanians and their roads.

I don't know where all the money from taxes and tourists goes in Costa Rica, but the booty is not invested in the roads.

The road was paved in Panama just like the Pennsylvania two lane blacktop that runs through the hills outside of Williamsport, PA. Santa Catalina is a small, former fishing village turned Scuba Center, where white folk come to dive and surfers come to get tubed on a reef break.

Santa Catalina is a village of 300 souls with two mini markets, a growing church population, ten hotels, a bunch of hostels and three dive shops. There is a bakery and there is a good library started up by a well-read eccentric gringo.

The bakery is run by a Spaniard married to a French pastry. They rise early and always look tired. You have to reserve muffins at the bakery because they always run out. "Zee Germans," Paulo said and looked over his shoulder as if there could possibly be a German who came through the back and was standing in the kitchen, "Zey are zee worst. They vant to buy all my mu-feen!" I tell them, "No. You may 'ave two of each."

I dug Paulo's attitude. He was not there to make a bunch of money or get up any earlier to make more muffins. He refused to be handcuffed to capitalism. He put a cap on muffin buying in this little world on the edge, next to the ocean in Panama, two hours from nowhere.

I witnessed him refusing muffins to an Australian a few weeks later. After he sent the would-be glutton on his way, he shook his head and we exchanged a knowing nod. "Can you bee-leeve zees people? Zey vant to buy all my mu-feen."

In any given hippy artist community there will be those that take the Jesus look, like Cat Stevens before Islam: a wealth of masculine chin hair accompanied by shoulder length weathered locks.

Our beach town of choice in Panama has three Jesus's. We are high on the Jesus scale for such a small a population. There is the Venezuelan Jesus and The Florentine Jesus and the third Jesus may just be the Florentine on laundry day. I swear I never figured it out.

Santa Catalina is where a fishing village used to be. Fishing villages are going extinct just like the fish they used to catch are going extinct. The Patagonian Tooth Fish aka Chilean Sea Bass, tuna and sharks in the Central Pacific, they are all but gone. Also going are the Leatherback Turtles, ancient beasts the size of a queen sized mattress. Check em' out on YouTube, because it is about the last place you can see them.

Fishing doesn't pay the bills. The one man on Homer's Boat with the darkness and the storm and the alcohol abuse and long nights under starry skies followed by the bumpy ride home is going the way of the buggy whip.

How can one man compete with a high tech, three team corporate flotilla complete with three helicopters and fifteen miles of nets?

Santa Catalina, the former Fishing Village, is now Santa Catalina, Scuba and Surf Village. The fishing boats are still moored but they don't go out so much without paying clients on board.

The day of the Divorce Mediation nothing happened, just another silent fart in the wind. She was not willing to accept less than fifty thousand dollars and a whole list of things I didn't have or didn't want to give. I assumed that my wife had the financial means at her disposal to not feel the pressure.

"Ok," I thought. Apparently she doesn't need the money yet. If she did need the money, then she would at least begin to negotiate.

She has made her decision and I have made mine.

Panama was not the place where I could find the internet connection and the beach culture I was looking for.

What about Venezuela? There are beautiful beaches in Venezuela and the American Dollar is super strong. I may not even need to work if I lived there. I could live off the little bit of money from the rent from the house in Bensalem and write full time.

Iris and I decided to go to Venezuela and look for the place that we both felt was our new home together.

Before we could leave for Venezuela we needed to sell my car and part with the remainder of our material possessions that would not make the trip.

We made a few lifelong friends during our month in Santa Catalina. Fabio is a Kuna Indian who rolled in to town with a Galician couple. He wore his hair long and his soul on his sleeve. He is guileless and beautiful in his way. He makes jewelry and travels around selling his art.

We made friends from, "Hello."

We exchanged pieces of our lives, a custom that links our lives together.

We also made friends with the Venezuelan Jesus. His name was Antonio and he travelled through Central America and Mexico making and selling jewelry by sitting on the corner with his wares on a cloth.

Chapter 16: Few Possessions.

We shed most everything: cool paper machete lamps and tiled mirrors, tools and drills, surfboards and my bicycle (Kuna bought the bicycle, a stripped down ten speed with one gear).

The car was the biggy. I planned on a friend coming to the border, signing the car over to him and he would in-turn sell the car and then send me the money minus his commission.

That was the plan, but I found out there was a lien on the car based on child support payments. I couldn't sell the car even if I wanted to pay for child support with the money. I thought the car was mine, but it sure felt like it belonged to someone else.

The Mitsubishi was in excellent mechanical condition, it was diesel and a stick, the price on the market would be about $4,000 and I would accept $3,500.

Now that I couldn't legally sell the car, I would have to go back to the border, first find, then climb another criminal ladder and sell the car to a chop-shop.

We arrived at the border town of Paso Canoas, (where I thought I would never have to return to) at sunset. I parked in front of the car wash and asked the attendant to give my car a wash and did he know of anyone who buys cars.

This was guy number one, just like the illegal stamp and any other criminal games one desires to engage in: if you are a stranger and know nothing: you go low on the totem pole and work your way up to the big dogs.

The car wash attendant directed me to a restaurant just down the street. I went there and spoke with Dom Emilio. He was a mid-40's guy who dressed well for being at the border. I explained the car had a lien, I couldn't legally sell it, and the condition was tip top, "What could you offer me?"

He said that he just bought an illegal car so he couldn't use mine right now. I asked him who may be interested and he pointed me down the road.

I was going to the third guy in the chain.

The chop shops and part stores were closing for their Friday night. We had tickets to fly to Venezuela on Tuesday and it was a one day trip to Panama City.

With everything closed on Sunday, we had Saturday to sell the car or abandon it.

Saturday morning I went out and sold that car for $600. It was my best offer and I was happy to get it. The parts guy will make a few thousand off the car. He provided a service. It was just more money that was gone.

I was a teacher living in a modest suburb of Philadelphia with a minivan and three children. Now I am a criminal on the run who can find a chop shop in a border town.

The things I gained, the things I had lost.

Iris and I were off to find our life together. We couldn't return to the U.S. because Iris does not have a Visa, so that entire country was off the list.

Where would be our home?

Chapter 17: Chavez, I'm Home.

We arrived in Caracas from Panama. The flight along the coast of Venezuela was a paradise in aqua blue; mountains ran to the sea, white sand beaches lay like strips from an artist's brush.

I was carrying about $2500 in cash.

Venezuela is funny. The official exchange rate for dollars is about 5 Bolivars per $1. However, there is a black market for dollars where the rate is about 20 Bolivars per $1.

We arrived at the airport and Iris began with illegal activity. We needed to exchange some dollars, just enough to get us to Caracas where Iris knows a black market money exchanger.

Iris managed to get a baggage handler to exchange dollars at 10 to 1. The baggage handler was thrilled with the rate and we hired a Lincoln Navigator to drive us the 40 kilometers to a nice neighborhood in Caracas where the black market U.S. dollar exchange awaited us.

After the money exchange, we went to visit Iris' mother. We stayed with a friend of Iris for one night before we left for the beach to find our home at Puerto La Cruz.

Like all things touristic during the reign of Hugo Chavez, Puerto La Cruz went to the dogs. A formerly grand esplanade with immaculate gardens, where artists formerly sold their wares and handsome families dined at seaside restaurants, was now deserted. The restaurants were shuttered and the streets reeked of urine. We took one look at the beach and instantly knew this wasn't the place for us. The people didn't wear bathing suits, the beach was small, everything was used and dirty, even the ocean.

After less than 1 minute on the beach in the neighborhood of Lecheria, Iris and I decided this was not home.

The next day we ate empanadas as we boarded the high speed ferry that took us to Santa Margarita Island. Santa Margarita lies about 100 kilometers off the coast of Venezuela in the Caribbean.

White sand beaches, crystal blue water, cool shops and internet greeted us.

We could live here, there was a row of shops along the beach, there were waves to be surfed and because of the exchange rate on the black market, I could write full time and we could live off of the rent from the Bensalem house.

The deciding factor in our decision to leave Venezuela was the manner in which business was conducted. I was interested in bringing teachers from the U.S. to teach U.S. based students online.

To start and maintain a business in Venezuela, somebody gets paid-off, some activity is illegal and once a business or lifestyle is committed to illegal activities then at any given moment everything that you have worked for can be taken away.

I never want to have to commit myself to crime, no matter how innocuous. I certainly didn't want to have to explain to teachers that they needed to go to the black market to cash their paychecks.

As a small business owner, I found Venezuela to be too risky an endeavor to set-up shop. I understood how major corporations would hold-off on investment in a country like Venezuela with a socialist leaning president like Chavez.

Businessmen run for the hills.

Iris and I decided we would run for Puerto Escondido, Mexico.

We were fast running out of money. We had been travelling for the past 6 weeks. We stayed super cheap and lost weight but money flies regardless with plane tickets and accommodations.

The bet on Mexico was all or nothing. We would arrive on fumes and hope for the best.

We needed to find a home.

"Hail Mary, full of grace…"

Chapter 18: Arriving to Puerto.

This travelling around business is painted as glitz and glamour but ask anyone who has been on the road for more than a month and they will tell you the same: There is no place like home. Travelling is unfamiliar beds and pillows. Travelling puts ya' off yer' feed, simple common meals for me were bananas and nuts and yogurt, when travelling; you eat what is at hand.

We were tired and nervous and we wanted to find a place to live, a home.

We arrived at Benito Juarez International Airport in Mexico City in the small hours of the night. We lay on the cold concrete benches for a few hours of restive sleep.

At 7am the local airline that services Puerto Escondido opened for business. The problem was our lack of funds and excess luggage. The excess luggage cost more than the fares so that put the flight option to bed. We would take a bus.

We took a taxi to the bus terminal and found that the only bus to Puerto was leaving at 6pm that night. We had to spend the day in the bus terminal, alternately taking walks and standing outside to smoke a cigarette.

The bus ride was a 17 hour affair of stops every three hours at distant weigh stations to drop off and pick up other bleary eyed travelers.

We arrived in Puerto at 11am the next morning, unpacked our excessive luggage that barely fit into the taxi and asked the driver to take us to a cheap hotel. Fortunately, the driver took us to a hotel that was pricier than we wanted; it was a gringo trap on the wide boulevard that affronts the beach and afforded us the luxury of a shower, a clean bed and was still only $25 a night.

Chapter 19: Dream House.

We found a map and spoke with a bartender and the hotel desk clerk about housing. The next day, we would start walking to find an apartment.

We set off in the early morning and walked in the blazing sun, after an entire day in the heat, we were exhausted and ready to disagree about anything based on hunger and lack of energy.

The following day we walked the neighborhood closer to the hotel. I asked everyone I saw if they knew of an apartment. We passed a Gringo couple as they were getting out of their car. I introduced myself and asked if they knew of any apartments and the misses said, "Sorry no."

Iris and I continued down the hill when Ann called back to us, "John, I do know of a place." She remembered my name. That is a good sign.

Her husband is Alex, an Englishman in his 70's, a former Pro Rugby player and body builder, a butterfly expert, master framer and part time artist. He took us to a small house their daughter owns on the next street.

We were one block from the beach on the rise of a hill, the large green outer doors opened to reveal a view of the ocean from the front seat of the car of life. There was no better view of the water.

The house was small and newly painted with all new furnishing and pots and pans and sheets and an immaculate bathroom. It was a small studio but big enough for us. The front porch of the house vertically dropped into the pool, eight feet below. The in-ground pool was bigger than the house.

To say that we fell in love with the place is weak. It was perfect, a brand new home with a world class view, one block from the ocean with air conditioning.. Pinch me, pinch me. We had shared a communal bathroom in Panama and hadn't had a refrigerator in our lives for two months.

The rent was a little more than we could afford but it was dream house one block from of the beach.

We paid the months' rent and put down our security deposit.

We now had a place to live and cook and write and paint.

*The Divorce proceeding was at a standstill because I had left the country and could not be served. Dan Knight couldn't take it anymore. Soledad had been telling him for two years that she was either Divorced or the Divorce was happening soon. He wanted out of the relationship with Soledad. He worried who would take care of the kids.

Chapter 20: May 2013, Nursing Pop.

He had been sick with cancer for the two years since I moved to Costa Rica. I never thought I would see him alive again. The Child Support kept me in Costa Rica. Without the written permission of my wife, I would have to post 15 months of Child Support to receive permission to leave Costa Rica. Since the Child Support jumped to $1,600 a month, I would have to come up with $24,000 in cash. I didn't have that money. If my father died while I was in Costa Rica, I would not be able to attend the funeral and be with my mother. I accepted that I would never see my parents again when I entered Costa Rica. I avoided that scenario when I escaped from Costa Rica in 2012.

In April of 2013, I left Iris and Mexico to be with my family. My father was in the ICU and he may not be coming out alive.

I flew to the U.S. from Mexico and spent two months with my parents.

Pop

Joseph Patrick Murphy, "Pop," worked until he was 82 years old. He drove himself to cancer treatments and only stopped working when he just couldn't walk to the truck to go to work no more.

I arrived to his hospital bed after 26 hours of travel. I had not seen Pop in two years. We had communicated through email and phone calls during that time, but I hadn't seen him.

I went into the room and wasn't sure the person in the bed was my father. This was a bald old man who was ghost white, frightened and surely dying.

I held Pop's hand and he smiled. He was relieved. He knew he was on his way out.

He was in pain that night, and at one point I wished the Lord to take him.

Pop recovered his strength to leave the hospital and since I would be home to help my mother, he would avoid going into Rehab surrounded by strangers. Pop wanted to "go out" in his own bed. He didn't want to spend another minute in the hospital. Nobody does, especially when you're dying.

I lived with my parents for those two months. I just helped that little bit that they needed. I took Pop out for rides in the city, his old stompin' grounds. We bought hot sausage sandwiches and made the rounds of classic bakeries to buy thick crème filled donuts and German sticky buns.

We went to the back alley kielbasa store in the polish section of Philadelphia and sliced thick raw sandwiches using his penknife. We ate in the truck and he told me stories of where he loved, fought, drank and rode horses.

In the late 1940's Pop was in his late teens. He rode horses as transportation. He was at a bar near PennyPack Park and then he took off on his horse for home.

He was galloping north on Frankford Avenue when he found himself falling straight down into a six foot wide trench that was dug into the street to repair a sewer pipe. From a dead gallop to down a hole, his chaps scraped the sides and the horse landed standing up right with Pop sitting astride. The trench was about 12' deep and Pop stood on the horse's back and climbed out and went to the bar on the next corner to have a drink and wait for the consequences. Turns out, Pop new the streets department foreman who had called the fire department to extricate the horse in the hole. The foreman looked at Pop as he walked up to the scene and said, "Murphy, I should a known it was you."

Pop and I sat on our back porch during the time before he died. It was late at night, 10pm or so and we talked about horses and the rodeo. I said, "Why don't we bring the saddle up from the basement?"

His saddle, the saddle that his father bought from him when he was twelve years old, was waiting in the basement. In the rodeo pics that we have of my father, he is riding on that saddle, it's the only one he had his whole life. I said, "How many times have you carried that saddle in your life. It is only 30 feet away. Let me go get it and we can saddle soap it up."

I brought it up and sat saddle and stand in front of my old man. He had tubes for oxygen and a walker but when I handed him the saddle soap he grew young and he told me this story:

In about 1946, he was rodeoing with a guy by the name of Morgan. Morgan used to say, "You got it in the hands Murph. You gotta' have it in the hands."

Morgan was referring to the ability to manage a horse in the harness, whether for the races or transportation. Ya' gotta' have it in the hands. A driver needs to feel the horses' mouth and gait through leather straps connected to a distant bit clenched between the horses' teeth. It takes a sensitive lover to control the motion of a beast by the slightest tension on a leather harness. Ya' gotta' have it in the hands. My father was proud that Morgan thought he had it in the hands.

Morgan and my father went to West Virginia to rodeo. They hooked up as a two man team. They switched shirts mid-way through so it looked like there were at least four guys. Morgan was a black guy and one of the few who rode. His partner was Joseph Murphy, Jr.

In 1947, rural West Virginia was not known for its liberal position on civil rights. We were still a full decade before Martin Luther King, Jr. would come knocking on the doors of moral justice.

Folk in West Virginia didn't much like the look of two cowboys from the city and one of em' a darkie at that. Pop didn't like the locals' opinion of his friend, so a bar fight ensued and the police came to save Pop and Morgan. Pop said he got thrown out of a window, just like in the movies.

He got outta jail and they made their way back to Philadelphia. He was fightin' for civil rights in word and deed when MLK, Jr. was in high school.

So those two months before Pop died, I was able to spend with him and my mother. We ate and talked and I gardened and hooked his horse and we enjoyed what all we had left of this life together.

I was blessed to be able to have this time to be with my parents and allow my father to spend his last days in his home.

My father and mother called to speak with my children during the last two months of his life. Once my mother got through but the next week and forever after…nobody answered the phone.

My wife's prediction became reality: My father never did see his grandchildren again.

RIP. JPM. 19 July 1931…25 July 2013.

Chapter 21: Hidden Betrayal, the Last Piece of the Puzzle.

While nursing my father in May 2013, a person claiming to be my wife's ex-boyfriend emails me. He wants me to pay him $23,000 that he says my wife owes him and now I owe him. He also wants me to start paying child support. He is tired of supporting my children and the lies from my wife. He sends pictures of my children and information that will help me, "get my children back." In short, proof of illegal activity that my wife and her lawyer were involved in.
I tell him I am not interested. I had been playing reindeer games long enough.

In February of 2014, he sends me nude pics of my wife and the information that my divorce has been finalized. I thank him for the divorce info and don't mention the pics.

He emails me again and starts telling me the whole story of his relationship with my wife and her lying ways. He too was manipulated for a few years. He wants to know about me as well, so he can sort out the lies from the truth about what he thought was his relationship with my wife. He, like me, is looking for some truth and closure.

After four years of trying to understand my wife's motivation, four years of introspective soul searching for all the causes of the mess that my life had become, I had finally found the last piece of the puzzle.

"Oh," I say, slapping myself on the forehead, "she had a boyfriend."

I was yoked down under the ignorance of hidden betrayal. I operated on a reality that wasn't real. I didn't have all the information. My children too, are living a lie, their reality isn't real.

I now have a better understanding of what really happened over the course of the past four years. I read my actions in this book and it is no longer sad for me. I feel for the person that I was, the father whose children were kidnapped, but I accept what the universe has given and what the universe has taken away, knowing that everything is temporary and that the nightmares of today can change into the dreams of our future.

I will be reunited with my children. The Virgin promised me on that first pilgrimage. I am waiting.

Spiritual journeys transcend time trials. My children, like my father, although not with me, are very much a part of me; they are in every thought that crosses my mind, in every apple that I eat, and every word that I type here in Mexico, four years after the fact.

Afterword

In December of 2014, I saw the movie with Sally Field, "Not Without My Daughter." I then googled, "International Parental Kidnapping" and found this definition on the Department of Justice's website:

"Federal law prohibits a parent from removing a child from the United States or retaining a child in another country with intent to obstruct the other parent's custodial rights."

With all the new information from Dan Knight, I now knew my wife's intentions. What always felt like a kidnapping had a basis in law. I was always stuck on the fact that I drove my wife and children to the airport. How could it be a kidnapping if I let them go?

I did not know her intention. I was filled with new fervor to seek legal remediation from U.S. justice.

In short, I contacted, provided a timeline, emailed and interviewed with the following U.S. offices, each on more than one occasion, from January 2015 until May 2015:

The U.S. Consulate in Costa Rica, The State Department Costa Rican Caseworker of Children's Issues, The U.S. Attorneys' Office in Philadelphia, The Department of Homeland Security, The National Center for Missing and Exploited Children, Local Law Enforcement where we resided in Bensalem, the FBI Philadelphia Office, my U.S Congressman who referred the case to the FBI Washington Liaison and the Committee for Missing and Exploited Children plus a few legal experts for good measure.

If the FBI would open a case, then I could have my children listed on the National Center for Missing and Exploited Children website. I did not expect helicopters and Navy SEALS. My hope was that someday when Sean, Ted or Elizabeth googled their own name, that their picture would appear as victims of International Kidnapping and that they would have access to the truth about their lives and their father.

Although sympathetic to my case, the FBI Agent could not act without my wife breaking a Custody Order. However, there is no possibility for me to get a Custody Order because the children have not resided in Pennsylvania for more than six months.

I would have needed to apply for custody in 2011 but my wife never cut off contact, so I had no reason.

Without my ex-wife breaking a Custody Order, there was no crime in the eyes of the law and proving her "intention to kidnap," was just about impossible.

"Isn't custody inherent?" I thought. It is not.

Isn't the fact that she clearly "obstructed my custodial rights," proof of her intention. It is not.

There is no remediation in the U.S. Justice System.

I have heard a thousand doors close over the past five years, another door will open.

I started this book calling out to my children and I end by doing the same:

"Ian, Ben and Hannah, I am hoping you will hear me."

John P. Murphy
Mexico, 2015

Acknowledgements

This book would not have been possible without Iris. She is my dream that has become my reality.

My parents helped me write this story from the beginning.

I would like to thank Paul, Jackie and Ava Garofano for their faith and support.

Andre Floyd, a former student of mine, who was my teacher from the first day I met him, provided timely advice and encouragement when I most needed it. He is a son whose mother took him from his father. He lent me a perspective on what my children were experiencing.

David Thelin, from the Committee for Missing Children has provided invaluable information and support. He knows more about Family Abduction from 20 years of helping families than all the other people I spoke with put together.

To be Released in Fall 2015:

Parents' Night

a novel

by John P. Murphy.

When was the last time you experienced a fistfight?

How did you feel?

Explore Urban Unrest and the fears that motivate decisions for the players in a moderately corrupt urban charter school.

Written as the intersecting stories of administrators, teachers, students and parents, the book explores racial tension between the generation who will never forget separate water fountains and the generation that will only remember a black president.

Easy access porn has produced a sexual landscape where sexting and nude selfies desensitize and warp sexuality from 13 year olds to CEOs.

The stories are of people acting from common fear: of failure and success, the unknown and unemployment, from violence and the violent, from being considered either unwashed, unworthy or uppity; from losing your roots and maybe recognizing you never had any.

Taylor works, West waits, teachers tire and the admin abides in a week in the life of Global Citizens Technology Charter School.

About the Author

John P. Murphy wanted to be an English Teacher. When he graduated university with a teaching degree, he realized he had nothing of value to teach anyone.

He waited tables from hippy coffee shops in Boston to fine dining in NYC.

He began his teaching career in Cairo and grabbed a cultural hold on 19 countries and three more languages before he began his career as an Urban Educator in Philadelphia.

When his wife kidnapped his three young children and moved to Costa Rica, he drove them all to the airport.

He lives in Puerto Escondido, Mexico, with Artist Iris Burchi. He loves, writes, reads, surfs, runs, swims, paints and chases butterflies.

Visit: www.murphyjohnp.com

Follow the Facebook Fan Page: Time Capsule of a Costa Rican Kidnapping.

Made in the USA
Middletown, DE
03 July 2015